D1243845

BIBLIOGRAPHIES *of*
MODERN AUTHORS
(Second Series)

To

ROGER INGPEN

BIBLIOGRAPHIES OF
MODERN AUTHORS
(Second Series)

JOHN DAVIDSON
ERNEST DOWSON
KATHERINE MANSFIELD
ALICE MEYNELL
WALTER PATER
FRANCIS THOMPSON

Compiled and Edited by
C. A. and H. W. STONEHILL

JOHN CASTLE

7 HENRIETTA STREET STRAND LONDON

FOLCROFT LIBRARY EDITIONS / 1972

Library of Congress Cataloging in Publication Data
Main entry under title:

Bibliographies of modern authors.

    Most of the material in the first series originally
appeared in The Bookman's journal.
    Compilers: 1st ser., H. Danielson; 2d ser., C.A. and
H.W. Stonehill.
    CONTENTS: 1st ser. Max Beerbohm. Rupert Brooke.
Hubert Crackanthorpe. Walter De La Mare. John Drink-
water. Lord Dunsany. James Elroy Flecker. George
Gissing. Francis Ledwidge. Compton Mackenzie. John
Masefield. Leonard Merrick. Richard Middleton. Arthur
Symons. Jugh Walpole. [etc.]
1. English literature--19th century--Bibliography.
2. English literature--20th century--Bibliography.
3. English literature--Bibliography--First editions.
I. Danielson, Henry, ed. II. Stonehill, Charles
Archibald, 1900-   ed. III. Stonehill, H. Winthrop,
ed.
Z2013.B582   016.820'8'008   72-6241
ISBN 0-8414-0087-3 (ser. 1; lib. bdg.)

BIBLIOGRAPHIES OF MODERN AUTHORS

(Second Series)

JOHN DAVIDSON
ERNEST DOWSON
KATHERINE MANSFIELD
ALICE MEYNELL
WALTER PATER
FRANCIS THOMPSON

Compiled and Edited by
C. A. and **H. W. STONEHILL**

JOHN CASTLE

7 HENRIETTA STREET STRAND LONDON

Printed in Great Britain by
The Dunedin Press, Limited, Edinburgh
1925

PREFACE

OSCAR WILDE has generally been considered to be the central figure of the Eighteen Nineties. Indeed he was the most brilliant and most versatile writer of the period, though an unconscionable plagiarizer. Whistler has said much on the subject; more has been brought to light by students of the French writings of a slightly earlier period. But only recently have certain German scholars hit upon Wilde's greatest debt.

To Walter Pater belongs the credit of being the inspiration of the *fin-de-siécle*. From him Wilde drew both his æsthetic philosophy and artistic opinions. To *Marius the Epicurean, Dorian Gray* owes as great a debt as to *A Rebours*. In a word, the study of Pater is an essential basis for the study of the Decadence of the last century.

Ernest Dowson's poetry certainly compares well with Wilde's. John Davidson was the " Master's " equal in philosophy; Francis Thompson, the singer of the faith which was the toy of the Decadents.

A striking figure in contrast to her age was Alice Meynell. The guardian angel of Thompson and the patron and friend of many, she held herself aloof from the literary frenzy of the times. Hers was the softer touch of a mind above all affectation. No woman has ever written an essay to compare with *The Rhythm of Life*;

perhaps no man. To have written it in that time of intellectual attitudinizing was a feat of rare dignity.

And while we dwell upon the feminine influence in literature, it is relevant to mention the name of Katherine Mansfield. Of a quite different school, she has written stories of exquisite delicacy and refinement. She is the interpretess come from their own number whom women have awaited, the interpretess of the *ewig weibliche*.

These few remarks may serve to introduce this series of bibliographies of the works of six authors who have for some time been receiving attention from book-collectors—which attention, we venture to suggest, will be an ever increasing one. This volume is essentially of the same family as Mr. Henry Danielson's exceptionally well-received and pioneer work, *Bibliographies of Modern Authors*, 1921, published from *The Bookman's Journal* Office. John Addington Symonds was to have been here included, but the material has been excluded from this volume in view of the fact that a much more exhaustive bibliography, upon which Mr. Percy L. Babington has been for many years engaged, will appear in print shortly.

We are most grateful for the kind assistance of Messrs Wilfrid Meynell, Clement Shorter, Michael Sadleir, R. A. Walker, John Drinkwater, Victor Plarr, and Mrs. W. W. Vaughan; also for the co-operation of many members of the book-trade, Messrs. C. Bertram Rota, P. H. Muir, John & Edward Bumpus, Maggs Bros., Elkin Mathews, Walter T. Spencer, C. W. Beaumont, Davis & Orioli, P. J. & A. E. Dobell and J. G. Millward.

The reader is cautioned to remember that the measurements given are in every instance the maximum, and that pages often differ in size; that signature (J) is not used by printers. We submit the work as it stands, having made every effort to make it both accurate and exhaustive within its scope. Any corrections or additions which may be noted will be gladly received in care of the publishers.

C. A. S.

H. W. S.

August 10, 1925

CONTENTS

LIST OF FACSIMILES

JOHN DAVIDSON
1851—1909

THE NORTH WALL

BY

JOHN DAVIDSON

GLASGOW

WILSON & M^cCORMICK, Saint Vincent Street

1885

---

*Facsimile, actual size of type, of Title-page of No. 1.
(By courtesy of Mr. Clement K. Shorter).*

JOHN DAVIDSON

PART I: BOOKS AND TRANSLATIONS

(1)

[THE NORTH WALL: 1885]

The North Wall / By / John Davidson / [*Ornament*] / Glasgow / Wilson & McCormick, Saint Vincent Street / 1885 / *All rights reserved*

Collation: Foolscap octavo, 6½ × 4⅝; pp. 2 + 158 + 4; consisting of two pages Advertisements; Half-title, *The North Wall,* verso blank; Title-page, as above, verso blank; *To M.C.M.,* verso blank; Contents, verso blank; Text, pp. [9]—157, verso blank; Advertisements, 4 pp. Headlines throughout: verso, *The North Wall.;* recto, various.

Signatures: 1 leaf adv.; 4 leaves, not signed; A—I, by 8s; K, 4 leaves; 1 leaf adverts.

Issued in light grey wrappers lettered on front cover *The / North / Wall / By / John Davidson* / [Ornament] / *Glasgow / Wilson & McCormick, Saint Vincent Street;* on the back and inside wrappers, advertisements.

Published price, 1s.

(2)

[BRUCE: 1886]

Bruce / A Drama in Five Acts / By / John Davidson / Author of " The North Wall " / [*Floral ornament*] / Wilson & McCormick / Glasgow and London / 1886 / The Right of Translation and Reproduction is Reserved.

Collation: Foolscap octavo, 6⅞ × 4¼; pp. 164 + 4; consisting of a blank leaf, pp. [1—2]; Half-title, *Bruce,* verso blank; Title-page, as above, verso blank; Dedication; verso, *Dramatis Personæ*; Text, pp. 9—161, verso blank; Advertisements, p. [163], verso blank; 4 pp., blank.

Signatures: 4 leaves, unsigned; A—K, by 8s.

Issued in sky blue boards backed with white canvas; a white paper label reads, *Bruce / A / Drama.*

Published price, 2s. 6d.

A second issue of the first edition was published in 1893. The sheets of the present edition are bound up with the new title-page,—

Bruce / A Drama in Five Acts / By / John Davidson / Author of " The North Wall " / London / Elkin Mathews and John Lane / The Bodley Head, Vigo Street / 1893.

Some copies of the second issue carry *both* title-pages; some only the cancel page, and there are advertisements on the reverse of the Half-title; 16 pp. advertisements of *Elkin Mathews and John Lane, 1893,* are inserted. Binding as in the first issue.

(3)

[SMITH: 1888]

Smith / A Tragedy / By / John Davidson / Author of 'Bruce: A Drama' / Glasgow / Frederick W. Wilson and Brother / 1888

Collation: Foolscap octavo, $6\frac{3}{8} \times 3\frac{3}{4}$; pp. 72; consisting of Half-title, *Smith: A Tragedy*, verso blank; Title-page, as above, verso *(The right of translation and reproduction is reserved.)*; Dedication, verso blank; Fly-title, verso, List of Persons; Text, pp. 9—70; blank leaf, pp. [71—2]. Headlines throughout, *Smith*.

Signatures, 4 leaves, unsigned; A—D, by 8s.

Issued in parchment wrappers; on the front wrapper is reproduced the title-page.

Published price, 2s. 6d.

Some copies contain 10 pages of advertisements, reckoned in the pagination as 73—82; they are printed on paper of different quality than the text.

See note to *Plays: 1889*.

(4)

[PLAYS: 1889]

Plays. / Greenock: / John Davidson, 12 Brisbane Street. / 1889. / *All Rights Reserved.*

Collation: Crown octavo, $7\frac{5}{8} \times 5\frac{1}{8}$; pp. 176; consisting of Title-page, as above, verso blank; *Contents*, verso blank; Fly-title, verso, list of *Persons*; Text, pp. 7—175, verso blank. Headlines throughout : verso, according to the play; recto, Act and Scene.

Signatures : [A]—L, by 8s.

Issued in stiff cream-coloured wrappers lettered in red on front cover *Plays. / John Davidson.*

Contains *An Unhistorical Pastoral, A Romantic Farce,* and *Scaramouch in Naxos.*

A second issue of the first edition was published in the following year, when the sheets were transferred to T. Fisher Unwin, who issued it with a cancel title-page under the title of *Scaramouch in Naxos.* (Price, 5s.) A third issue, 1893, adds Elkin Mathews' and Lane's title-page and adv.

The three above plays, with the addition of *Bruce* and *Smith* were reprinted in 1894 by *Elkin Mathews and John Lane,* having by now acquired a frontispiece by *Beardsley.* (Price, 7s. 6d.) Issued in plum coloured buckram, and there was a special trial issue, of a very few copies, bound in white buckram.

(5)

[PERFERVID : 1890]

Perfervid / The Career of Ninian Jamieson / By / John Davidson / With Twenty-Three Illustrations By Harry Furniss / Perfervidum ingenium Scotorum / London / Ward and Downey /. 1890

Collation: Crown octavo, 7⅜ × 4⅞; pp. viii + 256; consisting of List of Advertisements, pp. [i—ii]; Half-title, *Perfervid,* verso blank; Frontispiece; Title-page, as above, verso blank; Contents, verso blank; Text, including Fly-titles, pp. [1]—254, imprint at foot, *Printed by R. & R. Clark, Edinburgh.*; Advertisements, pp. [255—6]. Headlines throughout; verso, *Perfervid*; recto, various. There is one illustration (at p. 134), and a frontis.

Signatures: [A], 4 leaves; B—R, by 8s.

Issued in light blue cloth lettered in gold: on back, *Perfervid* / —*the*— / *Career* / —*of*— / *Ninian* / *Jamieson* / [Ornament in black] / *With 23* / *Original* / *Illustrations* / *By* / *Harry* / *Furniss.* / *Ward &* *Downey*; on front cover, *Perfervid:* / *The Career of* *Ninian Jamieson.* / [line] / *John Davidson.* / *With 23* *Original Illustrations* / —*By*— / *Harry Furniss.* Figured end papers.

Published price, 6s.

A second (popular) edition was published in the same year, price 2s. 6d.

(6)

[THE GREAT MEN: 1891]

The Great Men / And / A Practical Novelist / By / John Davidson / Author of ' Perfervid ' 'Scaramouch in Naxos' Etc. / With Four Illustrations By E. J. Ellis / London / Ward & Downey / York Street, Covent Garden / 1891 / *All rights reserved*

Collation : Crown octavo, 7½ × 5; pp. viii + 284 + 4;
consisting of Half-title, *The Great Men / And / A
Practical Novelist*; verso, *Printed by Spottiswoode
and Co., New-Street Square London*; Frontispiece;
Title-page, as above, verso blank; *Note,* verso blank;
Contents, verso, *Illustrations*; Text, including Fly-
titles, pp. [1]—283, imprint repeated at foot, verso
blank; *By the Same Author,* pp. [1]—2; pp. [3—4],
blank.   Headlines throughout : verso, *A Practical
Novelist*; recto, various.

Signatures : [A], 4 leaves; B—T, by 8s.

Issued in red cloth, blind tooled on front and back covers,
and lettered in gold on back, *The / Great / Men /* [line]
/ John / Davidson / Ward / & Downey.   Figured end
papers.

Published price, 3s. 6d.

The Great Men is here first published; *A Practical
Novelist* is reprinted, (*The North Wall,* 1885).

(7)

[IN A MUSIC HALL : 1891]

In a Music-Hall / and Other Poems / By / John
Davidson / Author of " Scaramouch in Naxos "
" Perfervid " Etc / (Publisher's device) /
London / Ward and Downey / 12 York Street
Covent Garden W.C. / 1891 / [*All rights
reserved*]

Collation : Crown octavo, 7¾ × 5; pp. viii—120;
consisting of Half-title, *In a Music Hall*; verso

blank; Title-page, as above, verso, imprint of *Charles Dickens and Evans Crystal Palace Press.*; Contents, pp. [v]—vii, verso blank; Text, pp. [1]—120; imprint repeated at foot of page. Various headlines throughout. There are 33 pieces.

Signatures: [A], 4 leaves; B—H, by 8s; I, 4 leaves.

Issued in red cloth, lettered in gold on back, *In / A Music / Hall /* [line] */ John / Davidson / Ward / & / Downey*; on front cover, *In a Music Hall* [underlined] */ and Other Poems.* White end papers.

Published price, 5s.

(8)

[MONTESQUIEU: Persian Letters: 1892.]

Montesquieu / — / Persian Letters / Newly Translated into English / With Notes and Memoir of the Author / By / John Davidson / Author of " Scaramouch in Naxos," " Perfervid," &c. / With Portrait and Eight Etchings by Ed. De Beaumont. / Engraved by E. Boilvin / In Two Volumes / Vol. I [*II*] / London / Privately Printed / MDCCCXCII

Collation: 2 vols., Quarto, 7⅞ × 5¾.

Vol. I.; pp. 6 + xliv + 176 + 4; consisting of 3 blank leaves; ornamental Half-title, printed in three colours on Jap. vellum, *Persian Letters / Montesquieu / — / Volume the First,* verso, Notice of Limitation; Frontispiece; Title-page, as above, in red and black, verso blank; *Contents of Volume I,* pp. [v]—vii, verso blank; *List of Etchings,* verso blank; *Introduction,* pp. [ix]—xliii, dated and signed, *London, September, 1891.*; verso blank; Text, pp. [1]—175, verso ornament and imprint, *Chiswick Press:—C. Whittingham and Co., Tooks Court, Chancery Lane.*; 4 pp. blank. Headlines throughout; verso, *Persian Letters.*; recto, *Letter Number.*

Signatures: 3 leaves, unsigned; [a]—e, by 4s; f, 2 leaves; B—Z, by 4s; 2 leaves, unsigned.

Note: The List of Etchings is not reckoned in the pagination.

Vol. II.; pp. 6 + x + 208; consisting of 3 blank leaves; illuminated Half-title, as in vol. I., verso Notice of Limitation; Title-page, in red and black, as above, verso blank; *Contents of Volume II.,* pp. [v]—vii, verso blank; *List of Etchings,* verso blank; Text, pp. [1]—203, verso ornament and imprint; pp. [205—8], blank.

Signatures: 3 leaves, unsigned; [A]—DD, by 4s.

Issued in blue cloth with paper label on back reading *Montesquieu's / Persian / Letters / — / John Davidson / I [II] / With / Nine Etchings / —*; this is surrounded by a narrow red ruled border.

The edition consists of 500 copies, on hand made paper.

(9)

[Laura Ruthven's Widowhood: 1892]

Laura Ruthven's / Widowhood / By / C. J. Wills / Author of / " The Pit Town Coronet," " John Squire's Secret," " In and About / Bohemia,"

etc. / And / John Davidson / Author of
" Perfervid," " Scaramouch in Naxos," etc. /
Vol. I [*II, III*] / London / Lawrence & Bullen
/ 16 Henrietta Street, Covent Garden, W.C. /
1892.

Collation : 3 vols., post octavo, 7¼ × 4¾.

Vol. I. : pp. viii + 244 + 16 pp. adv.; consisting of
blank leaf, pp. [i]—[ii] ; Half-title, *Laura Ruthven's
Widowhood*; verso blank; Contents, verso blank;
Text, pp. [1]—243; imprint at foot, *Printed by
Cowan & Co., Limited, Perth.*; verso blank; 16 pp.
advertisements, dated *Autumn, 1892.* Headlines
throughout : verso, *Laura Ruthven's Widowhood*;
recto, according to the chapter.

Signatures : 4 leaves, unsigned; A—P, by 8s; Q,
2 leaves; 8 leaves, unsigned, of advertisements.

Vol. II. : pp. viii + 236 (similar to Vol. I.) + 16 pp.
advertisements.

Signatures : 4 leaves, unsigned; A—O, by 8s; P,
6 leaves; 8 leaves, unsigned, of advertisements.

Vol. III. : pp. viii + 220 (similar to Vol. I.) +4 + 16
pp. adv. The 4 pages after 220 are a part of Sig.
O; they contain notices of other works of Wills
(who seems, at this date, to be more popular than
Davidson). The letter " i " is missing from the
notice of "*Sibil Roso's Marriage.*" and the 16 pp.
adv. are dated *Autumn, 1892.*

Signatures : 4 leaves, unsigned; A—O, by 8s;
advertisements, 8 leaves unsigned.

Issued in green stamped cloth, blind tooled border on
front and back covers; lettered on back in gold, *Laura*

/Ruthven's / Widowhood / Vol. I. [II., III.] / C. J. Wills / and / John Davidson / Lawrence / & Bullen.
Greenish end papers with floral design.

(10)

[FLEET STREET ECLOGUES : 1893]

Fleet Street / Eclogues / *By* John Davidson /
Elkin Mathews / & John Lane / Vigo Street,
London / MDCCCXCIII

Collation : Foolscap octavo, 6¾ × 4¼; pp. viii + 108
(including adv.) ; consisting of blank leaf; Half-title,
Fleet Street Eclogues, verso bearing notice of
limitation of edition to 300 copies; Title-page, in
red and black, as above; verso blank; Contents, p.
[vii] ; verso blank; Errata Slip inserted, four lines;
Fly-title, *New Year's Day*, verso blank; Text, pp.
[3]—104 (with separate fly-title to each eclogue) ;
p. [105], blank; verso, Printer's device; pp. [107]
—[108], advertisements.   Headlines throughout,
verso, *Fleet Street Eclogues*; recto, sub-title of
contents.   There are seven Eclogues.

Signatures : 4 leaves, unsigned; A—F, by 8s; G,
6 leaves.

Issued in dark blue buckram lettered in gold on back
only, *Fleet / Street / Eclogues / By John / Davidson
/ Elkin / Mathews / and / John Lane*; top edges gilt.

Published price, 5s.

This volume was advertised by a four page subscription
form, printed in red and black : *Ready at Easter. Printed
by Miller & Sons; 300 copies on antique laid paper.
5s. net. Etc.*

(11)

[SENTENCES AND PARAGRAPHS : 1893]

Sentences / And Paragraphs / By / John Davidson / *Author of ' Scaramouch in Naxos "* &c. / μέγα βιβλίον μέγα κακόν / [*Publishers' device*] / London / Lawrence & Bullen / 16 Henrietta Street, Covent Garden / 1893

Collation : Foolscap octavo; 6½ × 4; pp. viii + 136; consisting of Half-title, *Sentences and Paragraphs,* verso blank; Title-page as above, in red and black, verso blank; Contents, pp. [v]—vii, verso blank; Text, pp. [1]—134, printer's imprint at foot; pp. [135]—[136] blank. Headlines throughout, *Sentences and Paragraphs.* There are eighty-two sketches.

Signatures : [A], 4 leaves; B—J by 8s; K, 4 leaves.

Issued in olive green cloth lettered in gold on back, *Sentences / and / Paragraphs / — / J. Davidson / Lawrence / and / Bullen.* White end papers.

Published price, 3s. 6d.

(12)

[A RANDOM ITINERARY : 1894]

A Random / Itinerary / By John / Davidson / [*Ornament*] / London / Elkin Mathews / and John Lane / Boston / Copeland & Day 1894

Collation : Foolscap octavo, 6⅞ × 4⅜; pp. viii + 206 + 2 + 16 pp. advertisements; consisting of Half-title, *A Random Itinerary*, verso bearing notice, *This edition is limited to Six Hundred Copies*; Woodcut frontispiece by Lawrence Housman; Title-page, as above, in red; verso blank; Author's Note, verso blank; Contents, pp. [vii]—viii; Fly-title, *The Thirty Eighth of March*, p. [1], verso blank; Text (with Fly-title to each section) pp. [3]—204; pp. [205]—[206] blank; pp. [1]—2 (included in Sig. N) describe books by same author; List of advertisements dated *September, 1893*, pp. [1]—15, verso, printer's ornament and imprint. Headlines throughout, verso, *A Random Itinerary*; recto, varying. There are six sketches.

Signatures : 4 unsigned leaves, A—N by 8s.

Issued in fawn coloured cloth lettered in gilt on back *A / Random / Itinerary / John Davidson / London / and / Boston / 1894*; two gilt ornaments on front cover, one (similar) on back cover. White end papers.

Published price, 5s.

Six hundred copies printed.

(13)

[BALLADS & SONGS : 1894]

Ballads & Songs / [*Ornament*] / By / John Davidson / 1894 / London : John Lane / The Bodley Head / Boston : Copeland & Day / 69 Cornhill

Collation : Foolscap octavo, 6⅞ × 4¼; pp. II + vi + 136+16 pp. adv.; consisting of blank leaf; Half-title, *Ballads and Songs*; verso blank; Contents, pp. [v]

—vi; Text, pp. [1]—130; *Note* by the author, p. [131]; verso, printer's ornament; Errata Slip inserted, 2 lines; advertisements (part of signature I) 4 pp.; 16 pp. advertisements, numbered, dated *1894*. Headlines throughout; verso, *Ballads and Songs*; recto, title of the poem. There are 25 poems.

Signatures: 4 leaves, unsigned; A—H, by 8s; I, 4 leaves; 8 leaves of advertisements, unsigned.

Issued in dark blue buckram, lettered in gold: on back, *Ballads / and / Songs / John / Davidson / The / Bodley Head / and / Boston*; on front cover, *Ballads & Songs / [Ornament] / By / John Davidson.*

Published price, 5s.

(14)

[BAPTIST LAKE : 1894]

Baptist Lake / By / John Davidson / Author of / " Perfervid," " Scaramouch in Naxos," / " The Great Men," Etc. / London / Ward and Downey Limited / 12 York Street Covent Garden WC / 1894

Collation: Post octavo, 7⅜ × 5; pp. viii + 352; consisting of Half-title, *Baptist Lake*; verso, *By the Same Author*; Title-page, as above; verso, *Printed by Kelly and Co. Limited, 182, 183 and 184, High Holborn, W.C., and Middle Mill, Kingston-on-Thames.*; Contents; verso blank; Fly-title, *Baptist Lake*; verso blank; Text, pp. [1]—351; p. [352], Notice by the Author. Headlines throughout, *Baptist Lake.*

Signatures: four leaves, unsigned; 1—22, by eights.

Issued in blue buckram lettered in gold on back, *Baptist / Lake /* [line] */ John / Davidson / Ward / and / Downey / Limited.* On front cover, *Baptist Lake /* [line]. Grey end-papers, with floral design.

Published price, 3s. 6d.

(15)

[EARL LAVENDER : 1895]

A Full and True / Account of the / Wonderful / Mission of Earl / Lavender, Which / Lasted One Night / and One Day : / With a History / of the Pursuit of / Earl Lavender / and Lord / Brumm By Mrs / Scamler and / Maud Emblem. / By / John Davidson. / With a Frontispiece / By / Aubrey Beardsley. / London : 12 York / Buildings, Adelphi : / Ward & Downey, / Limited. / 1895

Collation : Crown octavo, 7¾ × 5⅛; pp. xii + 292; consisting of Half-title, *Earl Lavender*; verso, *By the Same Author*; Frontispiece, signed on plate, *Aubrey Beardsley*; Title-page, as above, in red and black; verso, Poem, in five stanzas; p. [v], quotation from Gower; verso blank; Note, pp. [vii]—x; Contents, pp. [xi]—xii; Text, pp. [1]—290; imprint, *Colston and Company, Printers, Edinburgh* at foot; pp. [291]—[292], *Books by John Davidson.* There are headlines throughout, italicized, *Earl Lavender.* Signatures : a, 4 leaves; b, 2 leaves; A—S, by 8s; T, 2 leaves.

Issued in light blue buckram, lettered in gold on back, *Earl / Lavender / John / Davidson / Ward & Downey*

/ *Limited.*; on front, *A Full and True Account / of the Wonderful Mission / of Earl Lavender, Which / Lasted One Night and / One Day / John Davidson.* Plum coloured end papers.

Published price, 3s 6d.

(16)

[St. George's Day : 1895]

St. George's Day / A Fleet Street Eclogue / By / John Davidson / New York / John Lane / Brevoort House / 1895

Collation : Post octavo, $7\frac{1}{2} \times 4\frac{7}{8}$; pp. 16; consisting of Title-page, as above, verso *Copyright, 1895 By John Lane*; Text, pp. [3]—16. Headlines throughout : verso, *St. George's Day*; recto, *A Fleet Street Eclogue.*

There are no signatures, the book consisting of but one sheet.

Issued in pale orange wrappers; on the front cover is reproduced the title-page.

This pamphlet antedates by some four months the *Second Series of Fleet Street Eclogues,* in which it is reprinted.

(17)

[A Second Series of Fleet Street Eclogues : 1896]

A Second Series of / Fleet Street Eclogues / [*Ornament*] / By / John Davidson / 1896 /

London John Lane / The Bodley Head / New York Dodd Mead / and Company

Collation : Foolscap octavo, 6¾ × 4⅜; pp. viii + 104 + 16 pp. adv.; consisting of blank leaf; Half-title, *A Second Series of / Fleet Street Eclogues*; verso, notices *By the same author*; Title-page, as above; verso, notice of *Copyright*, etc. and imprint, *J. Miller and Son, Printers, Edinburgh*; Contents, verso blank; Fly-title, *All Hallow's Eve*, p. [1]; verso blank; Text (with fly-title before each Eclogue) pp. [3] —101; verso blank; pp. [103—104], blank; advertisements of John Lane, dated *1895* on the second page, 16 pp. Headlines throughout : verso, *Fleet Street Eclogues*; recto, varying with the text. There are five Eclogues.

Signatures : 4 leaves, unsigned; A—F, by 8s; G, 4 leaves; 8 leaves of advertisements.

Issued in dark blue buckram lettered in gold : on back, *Fleet / Street / Eclogues* / [Two ornaments] / *John / Davidson / The / Bodley Head / and / New York*; on front cover, *A Second Series of / Fleet Street Eclogues* / [Ornament] / *By / John Davidson.*

Published price, 4s 6d.

St. George's Day appeared as a separate title, *New York, 1895,* and is here reprinted.

(18)

[Coppée : For the Crown : 1896]

For the Crown / A Romantic Play, In Four Acts / Done Into English By / John Davidson / From

/ François Coppée's " Pour La Couronne " / and Presented at / The Lyceum Theatre / on / Thursday, February 27th, 1896 / [*Ornament*] / London / The Nassau Press / 60 St. Martin's Lane, Charing Cross / 1896 / *Copyright*

Collation : Demy ·octavo, 8½ ×5¾; pp. 60; consisting of Half-title, [Ornament] / *For the Crown* / [Ornament] ; verso blank; Title-page, as above, verso, *Nassau Steam Press, Limited, 60 St. Martin's Lane, London, W.C.*; *The Persons of the Play*, p. [5], verso, *Synopsis of Scenery.*; Text, pp. [7]—58, p. [59], ornament and imprint, verso blank.

Signatures : [A], B, C, 8 leaves; D, 6.

Issued in blue-grey boards backed with brown; the front cover reproduces the title-page within thin ruled border, with the substitution of *Price One Shilling.* for *Copyright.*

Published price, 1s.

There is an Opera, *The Cross and the Crescent,* composed by Colin McAlpin (quarto, 16 pp., London, [1903]) founded on Davidson's version of *For the Crown.* This opera was produced by the *Moody Manners Opera Company, Ltd.*, in 1903.

(19)

[MISS ARMSTRONG'S & OTHER CIRCUMSTANCES : 1896]

Miss Armstrong's / And Other Circumstances / By / John Davidson / Methuen & Co. / 36 Essex Street, W.C. / London / 1896

c

Collation: Crown octavo, $7\frac{1}{2} \times 5\frac{1}{4}$; pp. viii + 248 + 40 pp. adv.; consisting of Half-title, *Miss Armstrong's / And Other Circumstances*, verso, *By the Same Author*; Title-page, as above; verso blank; Note of thanks, verso blank; *Contents,* verso blank; Text, pp. 1—[248], imprint at foot, *Billings and Sons, Printers, Guildford.*; Advertisements, dated *March, 1896*, pp. [1]—40, numbered. Headlines throughout according to the story. There are 10 stories.

Signatures: four leaves, unsigned; 1—15, by eights; 16, four leaves. Adv. 20 pp.

Issued in blue cloth lettered in gold on back, *Miss / Armstrong's / and Other / Circumstances / John / Davidson / Methuen.* Also in red cloth, lettered as above, with the addition of *Miss / Armstrong's / And Other / Circumstances / By / John / Davidson,* in gold on front cover. Only the copies bound in red cloth bear the advertisements.

Published price, 6s.

(20)

[NEW BALLADS: 1897]

New Ballads / By / [*Ornament*] / John Davidson / John Lane / The Bodley Head / London & New York / 1897

Collation: Foolscap octavo, $7 \times 4\frac{1}{4}$; pp. 112 + 12 pp. adv.; consisting of Half-title, *New Ballads,* verso, advertisements; Title-page, as above, verso Notice of Copyright; *Contents,* verso blank; Text, pp. [7]— 110; *Note,* p. [111], verso, publishers' device;

Advertisements, dated *1896*, 12 numbered pages. There are 17 ballads.

Signatures: A—G, by 8s; 6 leaves, adv.

Issued in blue buckram lettered in gold: on back, *New / Ballads / John / Davidson / John Lane / The / Bodley Head*; on front cover, *New Ballads / By /* [Ornament] */ John Davidson.*

Published price, 4s 6d.

(21)

[GODFRIDA: 1898]

Godfrida / A Play in Four Acts / [*Ornament*] / By / John Davidson / John Lane: The Bodley Head / New York and London / 1898

Collation: Foolscap octavo, $6\frac{7}{8} \times 4\frac{1}{4}$; pp. 4 + 124; consisting of Half-title, *Godfrida*, verso, *By the Same Author*; Title-page, as above, verso Notice and imprint, *University Press: John Wilson and Son, Cambridge, U.S.A.*; Text, pp. [1]—123, verso blank. Headlines throughout; *Prologue* pp. [1—5], thence, *Godfrida*.

Signatures: [1]—8, by eights.

Issued in blue buckram lettered in gold: on back, *Godfrida / John / Davidson / John Lane / The / Bodley Head*; on front cover, *Godfrida /* [Ornament] */ By / John Davidson.*

Published price, 5s.

(22)

[THE LAST BALLAD : 1899]

The Last Ballad / And Other Poems / By John
Davidson / London and New York / John Lane
/ 1899

Collation : Foolscap octavo, 6⅛ ×' 4⅜; pp. vi + 188;
consisting of Half-title, *The Last Ballad / And
Other Poems*; verso, *By the same Author*; Title-
page, as above, within narrow ruled border; verso,
Copyright, etc.; *Contents,* pp. v—vi; Text, pp.
1—187, verso blank. Headlines, various.

Signatures : three leaves; [1], seven leaves; "2",
eight leaves; the remaining sheets are unsigned.

Issued in maroon buckram lettered in gold : on back,
*The / Last / Ballad / John / Davidson / John Lane /
The / Bodley Head*; on front cover, *The Last Ballad /
& Other Poems* / [Ornament] / *By / John Davidson.*

Not published.

This trial issue was suppressed and the remainder
of the edition bound in blue buckram, uniform with other
of Davidson's books, and similar to this issue in other
particulars.

Published price, 4s 6d.

(23)

[SELF'S THE MAN : 1901]

Self's the Man / A Tragi-Comedy / By / John
Davidson / " Be your own star, for strength is

from within; / And one against the world will always win." / London / Grant Richards / 1901

Collation: Crown octavo, $7\frac{1}{2} \times 5$; pp. viii + 224; consisting of Half-title, *Self's The Man*; verso, top, *Books by John Davidson*; foot, the Notice, *This Play was completed in September, 1899. Acting rights and all other rights reserved.*; Title-page, as above, verso bearing the imprint, *London: Printed by William Clowes and Sons, Limited, Stamford Street and Charing Cross.*; Contents, verso blank; *Persons*, verso blank; [pp. vii—viii]; Text, pp. 1—221; verso, imprint repeated; pp. [223—4], blank. Headlines throughout, recto and verso, *Self's the Man*.

Signatures: [A], 4 leaves; B—P, by 8s.

Issued in green cloth lettered in gold on back, *Self's / The / Man / John / Davidson / Grant / Richards*. White end papers. There was a crimson dust wrapper.

Published price, 5s.

(24)

[THE TESTAMENT OF A VIVISECTOR : 1901]

Testaments / By John Davidson / No. I. / The Testament / of a Vivisector / London: Grant Richards / Henrietta Street, Covent Garden / 1901

Collation: Square octavo, $8\frac{3}{4} \times 6\frac{7}{8}$; pp. 30; consisting of Half-title, *The Testament / of a Vivisector*; verso, Other works by J. D.; Title-page, as above, verso, *Edinburgh: T. and A. Constable, (late)*

Printers to Her Majesty; *Note,* verso blank; Text, pp. [7]—27, verso blank; Advertisements, p. [29], verso blank. Headlines throughout, *The Vivisector.*

Signatures : [A], eight leaves; A2, four leaves; A3, two leaves; one leaf, adv.; the sheets are laid one within the other, with the exception of the adv.

Issued in grey wrappers, 8⅝ × 7⅛, lettered on front in red and black, *Price Sixpence net.* [underlined] / *Testaments / By John Davidson /* [Double rule] / *No. I. / The Testament of a / Vivisector /* [Double rule] / *London / Grant Richards / 1901.*

Published price, 6d.

(25)

[THE MAY BOOK : 1901]

The / May Book / Compiled by Mrs. Aria / In Aid of / Charing Cross Hospital / " The primal duties shine aloft, like stars; / The charities that soothe, and heal, and bless, / Are scattered at the feet of man, like flowers " / London / MacMillan & Co. Limited / 1901

Collation : *Large Paper Copy;* Royal quarto, 11¾ × 8¼; pp. xii + 222; consisting of Half-title, *The May Book;* verso, Statement of Limitation; Frontispiece; Title-page, as above, in brown and black; verso, *Printed by Ballantyne, Hanson & Co. At the Ballantyne Press; The First Word,* verso blank; *Authors and Artists,* verso blank; Contents, pp. ix—x; *List of Illustrations,* pp. xi—xii; Text, pp.

1—221; verso, *Printed by Ballantyne Hanson & Co. London & Edinburgh.*

Signatures : [a], 4 leaves; b, 2; A—U, by 4s.

Issued in vellum wrappers lettered in gold; lengthwise, on back, *The May Book*; on front cover, *The May Book* / Compiled by / *Mrs. Aria* / *in aid of the* / *Charing Cross* / *Hospital*; gilt design on front cover; pink ties.

Collation : *Small Paper Copy*; Large quarto, 11¼ × 9¼; Preliminary leaves are the same, omitting Notice of Limitation; Title, in black only; Text, pp. 1—164; 16 pp. advertisements.
Signatures : [a], 4 leaves; b, 2; A—U, by 4s, X; 2 leaves.

Issued in blue cloth, and in green cloth, with designs and lettering.   Published price, 10s.

Davidson has contributed *Song, In "La Reine Fiammette"*, p. 29 (L.P. Copy), p. 24 (S.P. Copy); there is a photograph, by Bassano, of the author.

The illustrations in the L.P. edition are not included in the signature, as in the case of the S.P., but are on special paper, though reckoned in the pagination.

(26)

[THE TESTAMENT OF A MAN FORBID : 1901]

Testaments / By John Davidson / No. II. / The Testament / of a Man Forbid / London : Grant Richards / Henrietta Street, Covent Garden / 1901

Collation : Square octavo, 8⅝ × 6⅞; pp. 32; consisting of Half-title, *The Testament / of a Man Forbid*, verso, Advertisement; Title-page, as above, verso, *Edinburgh: T. and A. Constable, (late) Printers to Her Majesty*; Text, pp. [5]—29, verso blank; Advertisements, p. [31], verso blank. Headlines throughout, *The Man Forbid*.

Signatures : [A], eight leaves; A2, eight leaves; laid one within the other.

Issued in grey wrappers, 8¾ × 7, lettered, in red and black, on front cover, *Price Sixpence net.* [Underlined] / *Testaments / By John Davidson* / [Double rule] / *No. II. / The Testament of a / Man Forbid* / [Double rule] / *London / Grant Richards / 1901*

Published price, 6d.

(27)

[THE TESTAMENT OF AN EMPIRE-BUILDER : 1902]

Testaments / By John Davidson / No. III. / The Testament of / An Empire-Builder / London : Grant Richards / Leicester Square / 1902

Collation : Square octavo, 8⅝ × 6⅞; pp. 84; consisting of Half-title, *The Testament of / An Empire-Builder*, verso and p. [3], advertisements; p. [4], blank; Title-page, as above, verso, *Edinburgh: T. and A. Constable, (late) Printers to Her Majesty*; Text, pp. [7]—81, verso imprint; pp. [83—4], blank. Headlines throughout : *Parable*, pp. [7]—14; thence, *The Empire-Builder.*

Signatures : [A]—E, by 8s; F, 2 leaves.

Issued in grey wrappers, 8¾ × 7; lettered on front in red and black, *Price One Shilling net.* [Underlined] / *Testaments / By John Davidson /* [Double rule] / *No. III. / The Testament of an / Empire-Builder /* [Double rule] / *London / Grant Richards / 1902*

Published price, 1s.

(28)

[THE KNIGHT OF THE MAYPOLE: 1903]

The Knight of the / Maypole / A Comedy in Four Acts / By / John Davidson / " Lord of May, and Lord of May again." / *An Unhistorical Pastoral.-* 1877 / London / Grant Richards / 48, Leicester Square / 1903

Collation: Crown octavo, 7½ × 5½; pp. 4 + viii + 100; consisting of Advertisements, pp. [1—3], verso blank; Half-title, *The Knight of the Maypole,* verso blank; Title-page, as above, verso bearing quotations and note signed *J.D.,* etc.; *Persons,* verso blank; *Scene.* and *Time.,* verso blank; Text, pp. [1]—97, verso [Ornament], *Chiswick Press: Charles Whittingham and Co. Tooks Court, Chancery Lane, London.*; pp. [99—100], blank. Headlines throughout, *The Knight of the Maypole.*

Signatures: [A], 6 leaves; B—G, by 8s; H, 2 leaves.

Issued in red boards lettered in gold: on back, *The / Knight / of the / Maypole / By / John / Davidson /* [Ornament]; on front cover, *The / Knight of the Maypole / John Davidson /* [Ornament]. There was a white dust wrapper.

Published price, 5s.

(29)

[A ROSARY : 1903]

A Rosary / By / John Davidson / London / Grant Richards / 48, Leicester Square / 1903

Collation : Square octavo, $7\frac{1}{2} \times 5\frac{1}{2}$; pp. viii + 212 + 4 pp. adv.; consisting of Half-title, *A Rosary.*, verso blank; Title-page, as above, verso, *Chiswick Press: Charles Whittingham and Co. Tooks Court, Chancery Lane, London.*; *Contents*, pp. [v]—vii, verso blank; Text, pp. [1]—211; imprint repeated at foot, verso blank; Advertisements, 3 pp., verso blank. Headlines throughout, *A Rosary.* There are 80 pieces.

Signatures : [A], 4 leaves; B—O, by 8s; P, 4 leaves (including the advs.).

Issued in red buckram lettered in gold : *A / Rosary / John / Davidson / Grant / Richards*; on front cover, *A Rosary / John Davidson.*

Published price, 5s.

(30)

[THE MEAL-POKE : 1903]

University of St Andrews / University College, Dundee / The Meal=Poke / Edited by /H. Bellyse Baildon, M.A., Ph. D., & R. Cochrane Buist, M.A., M.D. / for the Committee of / The Students' Union Bazaar / Dundee : James P. Mathew & Co. / 1903.

Collation : Quarto, 9⅝ × 7¼; pp. viii + 112 + 23 pp. adv. Davidson has contributed *The Dyer's Hand*, pp. 71—72.

Issued in brown cloth lettered and ornamented in green.

(31)

[A QUEEN'S ROMANCE : 1904]

A Queen's Romance / A Version of Victor Hugo's / " Ruy Blas " / Written for Lewis Waller / By / John Davidson / London / Grant Richards / 48, Leicester Square / 1904

Collation : Crown octavo, 7 × 5½; pp. 112 + 4 pp. advertisements; consisting of Half-title *A Queen's Romance*, verso bearing notices; Title-page, as above, verso *Chiswick Press: Charles Whittingham and Co. Tooks Court, Chancery Lane, London.*; *Persons*, p. [5], verso blank; Text, pp. [7]—111; verso, ornament and repetition of imprint; advertisements, 3 pp.; verso blank. Headlines throughout, *A Queen's Romance.*

Signatures : [A]—G, by eights; 2 leaves adv., unsigned.

Issued in red cloth lettered in gold; on back, *A / Queen's Romance / A Version / of / 'Ruy Blas' / John / Davidson / Grant / Richards*; on front cover, *A Queen's Romance / A Version of 'Ruy Blas' / John Davidson*; top edges gilt. There was a white dust wrapper.

Published price, 3s 6d.

(32)

[THE TESTAMENT OF A PRIME MINISTER : 1904]

The Testament of a / Prime Minister / By / John Davidson / ". . . . *To apprehend / The meaning of the adamantine reign / And power of Evolution in awful terms / of God and Judgement."* / London / Grant Richards / 48, Leicester Square, W.C. / 1904

Collation : Crown octavo, 7⅜ × 5½; pp. 104 + iv; consisting of Half-title, *The Testament of a / Prime Minister,* verso blank; Title-page, as above, verso *Chiswick Press: Charles Whittingham and Co. Tooks Court, Chancery Lane, London.*; Text, pp. 5—103, verso bearing ornament and imprint; Advertisements, pp. i—iv. Headlines throughout : verso, *The Testament of;* recto, *A Prime Minister.*

Signatures : [A]—F, by 8s; G, 6 leaves.

Issued in red buckram lettered in gold : on back, *The / Testament / of a / Prime / Minister / John / Davidson / Grant / Richards*; on front cover, *The Testament of / A Prime Minister / John Davidson.*

Published price, 3s. 6d.

(33)

[THE THEATROCRAT : 1905]

The Theatrocrat / A Tragic Play of Church / and Stage / By / John Davidson / London / E. Grant Richards / 1905

Collation: Crown octavo, 7½ × 4⅞; pp. viii + 196; consisting of Half-title, *The Theatrocrat / A Tragic Play of Church / and Stage,* verso blank; Title-page, as above, verso blank; p. [v], a Poem, verso blank; Contents, verso blank; Text, pp. 1—196; imprint at foot, *Plymouth, William Brendon and Son, Ltd., Printers.* Headlines throughout: verso, *The Theatrocrat*; recto, according to the Contents.

Signatures: [A], 4 leaves; B—M, by 8s; N, 4 leaves; N2, 6 leaves.

Issued in vermillion cloth lettered in gold on back, *The / Theatrocrat / John / Davidson / · E · Grant · / Richards.* Top edges gilt.

Published price, 5s.

(34)

[THE BALLAD OF A NUN: 1905]

The Ballad of a Nun / By John Davidson / With Illustrations by / Paul Henry / [*Ornament*] / John Lane: Publisher / London and New York / MDCCCCV

Collation: Sextodecimo, 5½ × 4½; pp. 44; consisting of Half-title, *Flowers of Parnassus—XXV / The Ballad of a Nun,* verso blank; Frontispiece, pp. [3—4]; Title-page, as above, verso *William Clowes & Sons, Ltd., London*; *List of Illustrations,* verso blank; Text, pp. 9—38 (the illustrations are reckoned in the pagination); Fly-title, *A List of Mr. John Davidson's Works,* p. [39], verso blank; Advertisements, pp. [41—4]. There are seven full page illustrations including the frontis. Headlines throughout, *The Ballad of a Nun.*

There are no signatures. Illustrations tipped in.

Issued in olive green cloth lettered in gold : on back, *F.P.* [in circle] / *The Ballad of a Nun* [lengthwise] / *John / Lane*; on front cover, *The / Ballad / of a / Nun*, within gold ornament. Also issued in leather binding. There was a pale green dust wrapper.

Published price : cloth, 1s; leather, 1s 6d.

(35)

[Holiday And Other Poems : 1906]

Holiday / And Other Poems / With a Note on Poetry / By / John Davidson / London / E. Grant Richards / 1906

Collation : Foolscap octavo, $6\frac{5}{8} \times 4\frac{1}{8}$; pp. 2 + vi + 156; consisting of blank leaf; Half-title, p. [i], *Holiday / And Other Poems*, verso, *Books By John Davidson*; Title-page, as above, verso bearing imprint, *Printed by Ballantyne, Hanson & Co. At the Ballantyne Press; Contents*, pp. v—vi; 2 line Errata Slip between pp. vi and 1; Fly-title, *Poems*, verso blank; Text, pp. 3—156; imprint repeated at foot.

Signatures : 4 leaves, unsigned; A—I, by 8s; K, 4, L, 2 leaves.

Issued in bright blue buckram lettered in gold : on back, *Holiday / and / Other / Poems / John / Davidson / E. Grant / Richards*; on front cover, *Holiday / And*

Other Poems / John Davidson; top edges gilt.   There was a white dust wrapper.

Published price, 3s 6d.

The question of issue is very often open when an *Errata* occurs. We have seen copies of this book without the slip, and with no trace of any alteration. These may be a first issue, or they may merely be lacking in this point. The copies in the Bodleian and British Museum Libraries *have* the slip which might be an indication of priority of issue.

(36)

THE TRIUMPH OF MAMMON : 1907

God and Mammon / A Trilogy / The Triumph / Of Mammon / By / John Davidson / With a Personal Note / By Way of Epilogue / London / E. Grant Richards / 1907

Collation : Crown octavo, 7⅝ × 5; pp. viii + 172 + 20 pp. adv.; consisting of p. [i], blank, verso *Books / By / John Davidson*; Half-title, *God And Mammon / A Trilogy / The Triumph / of Mammon*, verso blank; Title-page, as above, verso blank; *Contents*, verso blank; Fly-title, p. [1], *The Triumph of Mammon*, verso blank; *Persons*, pp. [3—4] ; Text, pp. 5—170; p. [171], imprint, *Plymouth / William Brendon and Son, Ltd. Printers*, verso blank; 20 numbered pages of advertisements, dated 1907. Headlines throughout; *The Triumph of Mammon*, recto and verso as far as the Epilogue (p. 151); thence, recto, *Epilogue*.

Signatures : [A], 4 leaves; B—L, by 8s, M, 4 leaves, M2, 2 leaves. Advertisements, 10 leaves.

Issued in olive green cloth lettered in gold on the back, *God and / Mammon / The / Triumph / of / Mammon / John / Davidson / ·E ·Grant· / Richards*; on the front, *The / Triumph of Mammon / John Davidson.* Top edges gilt.

Published price, 5s.

(37)

[MAMMON AND HIS MESSAGE : 1908]

God and Mammon / A Trilogy / Mammon and His / Message / Being the Second Part of / God and Mammon / By / John Davidson / London / Grant Richards / 1908

Collation : Crown octavo, 7⅜ × 5; pp. 2 + xiv + 176; consisting of a blank leaf; p. [i], blank, verso *Books By John Davidson*; Half-title, *God and Mammon / A Trilogy / Mammon and / His Message,* verso blank; Title-page, as above, verso blank; *Contents,* verso blank; *Note,* pp. ix—xiv; Text, including Fly-title, etc., pp. [1]—173, verso, *Plymouth William Brendon and Son, Ltd. Printers*; pp. [175—6], blank. Headlines throughout : *Mammon and His Message* to p. 142; thence, *Epilogue.*

Signatures : [A]—M, by 8s.

Issued in royal blue cloth lettered in gold : on back, *God and / Mammon / Mammon / and His / Message / John / Davidson / Grant / Richards*; on front cover, *Mammon / And His Message / John Davidson.* Top edge gilt. There was a tan dust wrapper.

Published price, 5s.

The third book was never published.

(38)

[THE TESTAMENT OF JOHN DAVIDSON : 1908]

The Testament / of / John Davidson / [*Ornament*] / London / Grant Richards / 1908

Collation : Crown octavo, 7⅜ × 5; pp. 148; consisting of p. [1], blank, verso *Books by John Davidson*; Half-title, *The Testament of / John Davidson*, verso blank; Title-page, as above, verso blank; Contents, verso blank; Fly-title, *Dedication*, verso blank; *Dedication*, pp. 11—32; Text, including Fly-titles, pp. [33]—[147], verso *Printed by William Brendon and Son, Ltd. Plymouth*. Headlines throughout : verso, *The Testament of John Davidson*; recto, various.

Signatures : [A]—I, by 8s. I2, 2 leaves.

Issued in bright red buckram lettered in gold : on back, *The / Testament / of / John / Davidson / Grant / Richards*; on front cover, *The Testament of / John Davidson*; top edge gilt.

Published price, 3s 6d.

(39)

[FLEET STREET : 1909]

Fleet Street / and Other Poems / By / John Davidson / [*Ornament*] / London / Grant Richards / 1909

Collation : Crown octavo, 7½ × 4⅞; pp. 152; consisting of Half-title, *Fleet Street / and Other Poems*; verso,

D

Books by John Davidson; Title-page, as above, verso bearing notice of copyright; *Preface,* verso blank; *Contents,* verso blank; Text, pp. [9]—[149] ; imprint at foot, *William Brendon and Son, Ltd. Printers, Plymouth*; pp. [150—1—2], blank.   Headlines throughout according to the poem.   There are twenty poems.

Signatures : [A]—I, by eights; K, four leaves.

Issued in bright green buckram lettered in gold; on back, *Fleet / Street / and / Other / Poems / John / Davidson / Grant / Richards*; on front, *Fleet Street / and Other Poems / John Davidson.*   There was a white dust wrapper.

Published price, 5s.

PART II:

BOOKS WITH AN INTRODUCTION
BY JOHN DAVIDSON

(40)

[FOSTER : Pictures of Rustic Landscape : 1896]
Pictures of Rustic / Landscape / By / Birket
Foster / With Passages in Prose and Verse /
Selected by / John Davidson / Author of ' Ballads
and Songs ' / With Portrait and Thirty Engrav-
ings / London / John C. Nimmo / 14 King
William Street, Strand / MDCCCXCVI

Collation : Demy octavo, 9½ × 6½; pp. xiv + 240,
  Introductory Note by Davidson, pp. [ix]—x.

Issued in olive green buckram.

(41)

[SHAKESPEARE : Sonnets : 1909]

The Complete Works / of / William Shakespeare
/ With Annotations and a General / Introduction
/ By Sidney Lee / Volume XXXVIII / Sonnets
/ With a Special Introduction by / John Davidson
/ and an Original Frontispiece by / F. Brangwyn
/ New York / George D. Sproul / 1909

Collation : Imperial octavo, 11⅛ × 8¼; pp. 4 + xxii
+ 144 + 4 pp. blank.   Davidson's *Introduction*
occupies pp. ix—xvi.

Issued in light green boards backed with dark green linen.
Paper label on back, [Double rule] / *Shake* / *speare* /
— / *Sonnets* / — / *Essay* / *By* / *John* / *Davidson* /
— / *Volume* / *XXXVIII* / [Double rule].

The English edition bears a slip on the Title-page,
covering the last three lines, which reads *London* /
George G. Harrap & Company / *15 York Street Covent*
Garden W.C.

ERNEST DOWSON
1867—1900

ERNEST DOWSON

(42)

[Book of the Rhymers' Club : 1892]

The Book / of the / Rhymers' Club / [*Publisher's device*] / London / Elkin Mathews / at the Sign of the Bodley Head / in Vigo Street 1892 / *All rights reserved*

Collation: *Large Paper Copy*; Quarto, 7⅜ × 5⅝; pp. xvi + 96; consisting of Blank leaf, pp. [i—ii]; p. [iii], blank, verso, Statement of Limitation; Half-title, *The Book / of / The Rhymers' Club*, verso blank; Title-page, in red and black, as above; verso, *J. Miller and Son, Printers, Edinburgh*; *The Rhymers' Club*, List of Members; verso blank; Notice of Sources, verso blank; *Contents*, pp. [xiii] —xv, verso blank; Text, pp. [1]—94; pp. [95—96], blank. Headlines, when occurring, *The Rhymers' Club*.

Signatures: 8 leaves, unsigned; A—M, by 4s.

Issued in blue boards with white parchment back lettered *The / Book / of the / Rhymers / Club*. A gold ribbon is attached as book-mark.

The edition is limited to 50 numbered copies.

41

Collation : *Small Paper Copy*; Foolscap octavo, 6⅜ × 5 ; collation agrees with that of the large paper copies.

Signatures : 8 leaves, unsigned; A—F, by 8s.

Issued in orange cloth; a paper label on back reads, *The Book / of the / Rhymers / Club / — / 5s. Net.*

Published price, 5s.

The edition is limited to 450 copies of which 350 were for sale.

Dowson has contributed six poems : *Carmelite Nuns of Perpetual Adoration*; *Amor Umbratilis*; *O Mors! quam amara est memoria tua homini pacem habenti in substantiis suis*; *Ad Domnulam suam*; *Vanitas*; *Villanelle of Sunset*. The two first mentioned are reprinted from *The Century Guild Hobby Horse,* Vol. vi, for 1891. The others appear here for the first time.

(43)

[A Comedy of Masks : 1893]

A Comedy of Masks / A Novel / By / Ernest Dowson / and / Arthur Moore / In Three Volumes / Vol. I [II, III] / [Publisher's device] / London / William Heinemann / 1893 / [*All rights reserved*]

Collation : 3 vols., post octavo, 7 × 4⅝.

Vol. I., pp. iv + 222; consisting of Half-title, *A Comedy of Masks*; verso, advertisements; Title-page, as above, verso blank; Text, pp. [1]—221, imprint at foot, *Billing and Sons, Printers, Guildford.*; p. [222], blank. Headlines throughout, *A Comedy of Masks.*

Vol. II.; collation agrees with Vol. I, with the exception that the Text is only 213 pages. There is a misprint *VOV II*, at the foot of p. 1.

Vol. III.; collation agrees with Vol. I, with the following exceptions : Text, pp. 1—204; imprint at foot; plus 16 pp. advertisements, dated *March, 1893*.

Signatures : *Vol. I*, two leaves, unsigned; 1—13, by eights; 14, seven leaves; *Vol. II*, two leaves, unsigned; 15—27, by eights; 28, three leaves; *Vol. III*, 2 leaves, unsigned; 29—40, by eights; 41, six leaves.

Issued in green cloth lettered in gold; on back, *A / Comedy / of / Masks / — / Dowson / and / Moore / Vol I* [II, III] / *Heinemann*; on front cover, *A Comedy of Masks*; there is an ornament in black in the centre of the front cover.

Published price, 31s 6d.

Popular editions in 1894 (one vol., price 6s) and 1896 (one vol., price 3s 6d); 1900 (price 1s 6d).

(44)

[A Basket of Primroses : 1894]

A / Basket of Primroses / with Love / and Best Wishes / [*Floral Design*] / London : / Ernest Nister / 24 St. Bride Street E.C. / New York : / E. P. Dutton & Co / 31 West Twenty Third Street. / Printed by E. Nister at Nuremberg / (Bavaria)

Collation : 32mo, size of reproduction; pp. 8, consisting of Title-page, as above; Text, pp. [2—8] ; at the foot of page 8, in microscopic characters is printed the signature, *E. Dowson.* Pages not numbered.

There are no signatures.

Issued in decorated board covers, the whole cut to the shape of a basket of flowers; on front cover, a basketful of flowers with the label *With Love*; back cover, ornamented with flowers, bears a scroll reading *To.........* / *From.........* Inside covers are blank. Stabbed with a metal clip.

This curious item was published in 1894 as a greeting card; the paper is of stiffer fabric than ordinary book-paper. It is likely that the Bodleian Library copy, 17078.g. (137), (which has, I believe, been swept up and lost since it was collated) is unique. There is no copy in the British Museum.

(45)

[SECOND BOOK OF THE RHYMERS' CLUB : 1894]

The Second Book / of / The Rhymers' Club / London : Elkin Mathews & John Lane / New York : Dodd, Mead & Company / 1894 / *All rights reserved*

Collation : *Large Paper Copy*; square octavo, 7½ × 5¾; pp. xvi + 136; consisting of pp. [i—iii], blank; verso, Notice of Limitation; Half-title, *The Second Book / of / The Rhymers' Club*, verso blank; Title-page, as above, in red and black; verso, *J. Miller and Son, Printers, Edinburgh*; The Rhymers' Club, Roll of Membership, verso blank; Acknowledgement of sources, verso blank; Contents, pp. [xiii]—xvi;

Facsimiles, actual size, of Title-page (top), and Covers (bottom), of No. 44.

Text, pp. 1—134; pp. [135—6], blank. Headlines, when occurring, *The Rhymers' Club.*

Signatures: 8 leaves, unsigned; A—H, by 8s; I, 4 leaves.

Issued in blue boards backed with parchment.

Of this edition there were printed 50 copies for England and 20 for America.

Collation: *Small Paper Copy;* Foolscap octavo, 6⅜ × 5; pp. xvi + 136 + 16 pp. adv.; collation follows that of the Large Paper edition; the title-page is printed in black only; at the end, 16 pp. advertisements, dated *1894.*

Signatures: 8 leaves, unsigned; A—H, by 8s; I, 4 leaves; 8 leaves, advertisements.

Issued in brown buckram lettered in gold on back, *The / Second / Book / of the / Rhymers' / Club / London / and / New York / 1894*

Published price, 5s.

Dowson has contributed six poems: *Extreme Unction; To One in Bedlam; Non sum qualis eram bonae sub regno Cynarae* (from the *Century Guild Hobby Horse,* Vol. vi, 1891); *Growth; You would have understood me, had you waited;* and *The Garden of Shadow.*

(46)

[Couperus : Majesty : 1894]

Majesty / By / Louis Couperus / Translated by A. Teixeira / De Mattos and Ernest / Dowson / [*Ornament*] / London / T. Fisher Unwin / 1894

Collation : Crown octavo, 7¾ × 5; pp. iv + 420; consisting of Half-title, *Majesty*, verso bearing Publisher's device; Title-page, as above, verso blank; Text, pp. [1]—419; verso, imprint, *The Gresham Press, Unwin Brothers, Chilworth and London.* Headlines throughout, *Majesty*.

Signatures : [1], two leaves; 2—27, by eights; 28, two leaves.

Issued in light blue cloth floreated with chocolate brown; lettered in gold on back, *Majesty* / — / *Louis* / *Couperus*; the same on front cover.

Published price, 6s.

(47)

[DILEMMAS : 1895]

Dilemmas / Stories and Studies In Sentiment / *The Diary of a Successful Man—A Case of* / *Conscience—An Orchestral Violin* / *Souvenirs of an Egoist—The* / *Statute of Limitations* / By / Ernest Dowson / London / Elkin Mathews / New York / Frederick A. Stokes Company / MDCCCXCV

Collation : Post octavo, 7½ × 4¾; pp. xii + 140 + 20 pp. adv.; consisting of a blank leaf; Half-title, *Dilemmas*; verso, *In Preparation*; Title-page, as above, verso bearing imprint, *J. Miller & Son, Printers, Edinburgh*; Dedication, *To Missie* (*A.F.*), verso blank; Notice of indebtedness, verso blank; *Contents*, verso blank; Fly-title, p. [1], verso blank; Text, pp. [3]—139, verso blank; 20 pp. advertisements, dated 1895. Headlines throughout; verso, *Dilemmas*; recto, title of the story.

Signatures : 6 leaves, unsigned; [A]—M, by 8s; I, 4 leaves, K, 2 leaves; 10 leaves advertisements.

Issued in French blue cloth, lettered on back in black, *Dilemmas / Ernest / Dowson / Elkin / Mathews*; on front cover, *Dilemmas*.

Published price, 3s 6d.

A Case of Conscience is reprinted from the *Century Guild Hobby Horse*, Vol. vi, for 1891; *The Diary of a Successful Man*, from *MacMillan's Magazine* for Feb., 1890; *An Orchestral Violin*, from *MacMillan's* for Aug., 1891 (there entitled, *The Story of a Violin*); *The Statute of Limitations*, from the *Hobby Horse*, No. 1, for 1893; *Souvenirs of an Egoist*, from *Temple Bar*, for Jan., 1888.

(48)

[Zola : La Terre : 1895]

La Terre / By / Émile Zola / Now First Completely Translated Into / English / By / Ernest Dowson / In Two Volumes—Volume I [II] / London : Printed by The Lutetian Society for / Private Distribution among its Members : / MDCCCXCV

Collation : 2 vols., Royal octavo, 8½ × 5¾.

Vol. I; pp. 2 + iv + 360; consisting of blank leaf; Half-title, *The Lutetian Society's Issues / IV / Émile Zola / La Terre*; verso, Notice of limitation of edition; Title-page, as above, in red and black; verso blank; Text, pp. 1—359, verso blank. Headlines throughout : verso, *La Terre*; recto, various.

Signatures : one leaf, unsigned; a, two leaves; 1—22 by eights; 23, four leaves.

Vol. II; pp. 2 + iv + 356; collation follows that of Vol I.

Signatures : one leaf, unsigned; a, two leaves; 1—22, by eights; 23, two leaves.

Issued in dark green cloth lettered in gold : on back, *Émile Zola / La Terre / Translated by / E. Dowson /* 1 [2] / [ornament] / *Lutetian / Society / MDCCCXCV*; ornament in gold on front cover; top edges gilt.

Of this edition 10 copies were printed on Japanese Vellum and 300 on hand-made paper.

(49)

[MUTHER : History of Modern Painting : 1895]

The History / of / Modern Painting / By / Richard Muther / Professor of Art History at the University of Breslau / Late Keeper of the Prints at the Munich Pinakothek / In Three Volumes / Volume One / [*Publisher's device*] / London / Henry and Co 93 St Martin's Lane / MDCCCXCV

Collation : 3 vols., Imperial octavo, 10¼ × 7.

Vol. I; pp. xii + 604; consisting of Half-title, *The / History of Modern Painting*, verso blank; Title-page, as above, in red and black, verso, Notice [see note] ; *Contents*, pp. [v]—xi, verso blank; Text, pp. 1—544;

Fly-title, p. [555], verso blank; Bibliography, pp. 557—586; Index of Artists, pp. 587—604; imprint at foot, *Printed by Hazell, Watson, & Viney, Ld., London and Aylesbury.* Headlines throughout : recto, chapter-heading; verso, *Modern Painting.*

Signatures : [a], two leaves; b, four leaves; 1—37, by eights; 38, four leaves; 39, two leaves.

Issued in blue cloth lettered in gold : on back, *The* [ornament] / *History / of* [orn.] / *Modern / Painting* / [orn.] *By / R. Muther* / [orn.] *Vol. I* [II, III] [orn.] / *Henry & Co.*; on front cover, *The History of / Modern Painting.* Small ornaments. Dark blue end papers.

The Note mentioned in the collation reads : *The translation of this volume was entrusted to Mr. Ernest Dowson, Mr. George Arthur Greene and Mr. Arthur Cecil Hillier. (Etc.)*

Volume One, only, is described as the subsequent volumes were the translation of Mr. Hillier.

Published price, 18s, each volume.

(50)

[VERSES : 1896]

Verses / By / Ernest Dowson / Leonard Smithers / Arundel Street : Strand / London W.C. / MDCCCXCVI

Collation : *Small Paper Copy;* Crown octavo, $7\frac{1}{2} \times 5\frac{3}{4}$; pp. xii + 60; consisting of half-title, *Verses / By / Ernest Dowson*; verso, Notice of limitation of edition; Title-page, as above, in red and black; verso, *Chiswick Press:—Charles Whittingham and Co. Tooks Court, Chancery Lane, London.; vitae summa brevis spem nos vetat incohare longam,* verso blank; *Contents,* pp. [vii]—viii; Preface, dated *Pont-Aven, Finistère, 1896.,* pp. [ix]—x; A Coronal, pp. [xi]— xii; Text, pp. [1]—57; verso, publisher's device and imprint; pp. [59—60], blank.

Signatures: [A], 6 leaves; B—D, by 8s; E, 6 leaves.

Issued in cream coloured parchment boards, lettered in gold on back, *Verses / By / Ernest / Dowson / Leonard /Smithers / 1896;* design in gold on front cover, signed *AB* in right hand lower corner.

Published price, 6s.

Of this edition, there were printed 300 numbered copies, on hand-made paper.

Collation: *Large Paper Copy;* Square octavo, $7\frac{3}{4} \times 5\frac{5}{8}$; pp. xii + 60; consisting of Half-title, *Verses / By / Ernest Dowson,* verso bearing Notice of limitation of edition; *Vitae summa brevis spem nos vetat incohare longam,* p. [iii], verso blank; Title-page, as above, in red and black; verso, imprint as in sm. paper; Contents, pp. [vii]—viii; the remainder of the volume follows the collation of the small paper copy.

Signatures: [A], 6 leaves; B—D, by 8s; E, 6 leaves.

Issued in parchment boards, lettered as the small paper copy. Japanese vellum end papers.

Of this edition, 30 copies were printed, on Japanese vellum.

The following poems are reprinted in this edition:
Nuns of Perpetual Adoration (*Century Guild Hobby Horse*, Vol. vi, 1891, and *The Book of the Rhymers' Club*); *Villanelle of Sunset* (*Rhy. Club*); *My Lady April* (*Temple Bar*, April, 1889); *To One in Bedlam* (*2nd Rhy. Club*); *Ad Domnulam Suam* (*Rhy. Club*); *Amor Umbratilis* (*C.G.H.Horse*, vi, 1891 and *Rhy. Club*); *Growth* (*2nd Rhy. Club*); *Non sum qualis eram bonae sub regno Cynarae* (*C.G.H.Horse*, vi, 1891 and *2nd Rhy. Club*); *Vanitas* (*Rhy. Club*); *O Mors! quam amara est memoria tua homini pacem habenti in substantiis suis* (*Rhy. Club*); *The Garden of Shadow* (*2nd Rhy. Club*); *Extreme Unction* (*2nd Rhy. Club*); *Impenitentia Ultima* (*Savoy*, No. 1, Jan. 1896).

Four Songs of Sorrow (*Opus 10*). *Poems of Ernest Dowson, Set to Music by Roger Quilter. London. Boosey & Co. 1908*, contains *A Coronal, Passing Dreams, A Land of Silence,* and *In Spring,* reprinted from this source, and now first set to music.

(51)

[Balzac: La Fille aux Yeux d'Or: 1896]

La Fille aux Yeux d'Or / [The Girl with Golden Eyes] / By / Honoré de Balzac / Translated By / Ernest Dowson / *With Six Illustrations Engraved on Wood by* / Charles Conder / [*ornament signed AB*] / Leonard Smithers / Royal Arcade: Old Bond Street / London W / 1896

Collation: Royal octavo, 10⅛ × 6½; pp. 4 + viii + 108; consisting of Half-title, *La Fille aux Yeux d'Or* /

E

By / Honoré de Balzac, verso blank; Frontispiece; Title-page, as above, in red and black; verso blank; *The Illustrations,* verso blank; *To Pierre Louys,* verso blank; *Translator's Preface* dated *Paris, December, 1895,* pp. [v]—vii, verso blank; Text, pp. [1]—107, verso blank; Illustrations as per table. Headlines throughout, *La Fille aux Yeux d'Or.*

Signatures: [A], 6 leaves, B—G, by 8; H, 6 leaves.

Issued in yellow cloth lettered in brown: on back, *La / Fille / Aux / Yeux / D'Or / H.de / Balzac / Translated / By / Ernest / Dowson / Leonard / Smithers and Co / 1896*; on front cover, *La Fille aux Yeux D'Or / — / Honoré De Balzac*; design in brown on lower cover; on back cover, Vignette in brown, signed *AB.*

Published price, 12s 6d.

A few copies only were issued as above; the remainder were suppressed, for though the gold cloth seemed appropriate to the title, the lettering does not show to advantage. The balance of the edition was issued in royal purple cloth lettered in gold.

(52)

[THE PIERROT OF THE MINUTE: 1897]

The Pierrot of the Minute / A Dramatic Phantasy / In One Act / Written by / Ernest Dowson / With a Frontispiece, Initial Letter, Vignette, and Cul-de-lampe by / Aubrey Beardsley / [*Ornament, signed AB*] / London / Leonard Smithers / Royal Arcade W / MDCCCXCVII / [*All dramatic rights and rights of translation are re-served*]

Collation: *Small Paper Copy*; Demy octavo, 9⅝ × 7¾;
   pp. 2 + 46; consisting of 2 pages, blank; Half-title,
   The Pierrot of the Minute, verso Notice of limitation
   of edition; Frontispiece, with tissue guard, p. [4];
   Title-page, as above, in red and black, verso,
   P. Naumann 65-71 Pentonville Road, London, N.;
   The Characters, verso blank; *The Scene*, verso blank;
   Text, pp. [11]—43; verso, Tail-piece; 2 pp. blank.
   Headlines throughout, *The Pierrot of the Minute*.

   Signatures: [A], B, & C, eight leaves.

Issued in olive green cloth lettered in gold on back, *The
/ Pier- / rot / of / the / Minute / By / Ernest /
Dowson / Illus- / trated / By / Aubrey / Beard- / sley
/ Leonard / Smithers / 1897.*; on front cover, design
in gold by Beardsley; lettering in gold, *The / Pierrot /
of / the / Minute / Written by Ernest Dowson / Drawn
By Aubrey Beardsley / Published By Leonard Smithers*;
designs in gold on front and back covers. Top edges
gilt.

Published price, 7s 6d.

The edition consists of 300 copies on hand-made paper.

Collation: *Large Paper Copy*; Large quarto, 10⅞ × 8¾;
   collation similar to Small Paper Copy.

   Signatures: [A]—F, by 4s.

Issued in vellum boards lettered in gilt as the small paper.
Japanese vellum end papers. Top edges gilt.

Edition limited to 30 copies printed on Japanese vellum.

There is a German edition limited to 800 copies on hand-made paper :

Ernest Dowson / Einen Augenblick Pierrot / Mit Zeichnungen / Von / Aubrey Beardsley / [*Ornament*] / München / — / Hyperion — Verlag / 1921

Collation : Demy octavo, 10⅞ × 6⅞. Parchment boards, gilt.

Set to music (1913) by Granville Bantock; with a note on Dowson by Rosa Newmarch.

(53)

[CHODERLOS DE LACLOS : Les Liaisons Dangereuses : 1898]

Les / Liaisons Dangereuses / or / Letters Collected in a Private Society / and Published for the Instruction / of Others / By / Choderlos de Laclos / Translated by Ernest Dowson / In Two Volumes / Volume One [*Two*] / With Fifteen Illustrations in Photogravure after Monnet / Fragonard fils and Gérard / London / Privately Printed / 1898.

Collation : 2 vols., Demy octavo, 8⅞ × 5⅝.

Vol. One; pp. xx + 298 + 2; consisting of Half-title, *Les Liaisons Dangereuses*, verso, Notice of Limitation; Frontispiece; Title-page, as above, verso blank; Notes and Preface, pp. [v]—xiii, verso blank; *List of Plates*, verso blank; *Contents of Volume the First*, pp. [xvii]—xx; Text, pp. 1—298; 2 pp., blank. Headlines throughout; verso, *Les Liaisons Danger-*

To the beloved hands
of W. H.

Alice

1914

CHILDHOOD

By
Alice Meynell

Published by B.T. Batsford. London

Facsimile, actual size of type, of Title-page of No. 93, with inscription in Author's hand on recto. (By courtesy of Mr. Wilfrid Meynell).

euses; recto, Letter Number. Illustrations, as per
list.

Signatures : ten leaves, unsigned; 1—18, by eights;
19, four leaves; one leaf not signed.

Vol. Two; pp. viii + 299—582 + 2; consisting of Half-
title, *Les Liaisons Dangereuses*, verso blank;
Frontispiece; Title-page, as above, verso blank;
Contents of Volume the Second, pp. [v]—vii, verso
blank; Text, pp. 299—581, verso blank; 2 pp. blank.

Signatures : four leaves, unsigned; 1—17, by eights;
18, five leaves; one leaf, unsigned.

Issued in blue boards with white linen back; lettering
in gold; on back, *Liaisons / Dangereuses / — / Choderlos
/ de / Laclos / — / Translated / By / Ernest Dowson
/ Vol. I.* [*II.*] / *Privately Printed / 1898*; on front cover,
Les Liaisons / Dangereuses.

Privately Printed Edition of 300 numbered copies.
Though there is neither publishers' nor printers' name
attached, it is known that this is the production of
Leonard Smithers.

(54)

[ADRIAN ROME : 1899]

Adrian Rome / By / Ernest Dowson and Arthur
Moore / Authors of " A Comedy of Masks " /
Methuen & Co. / 36 Essex Street, W.C. / London
/ 1899

Collation : Crown octavo, $7\frac{1}{2}$ × $4\frac{1}{2}$; iv + 364 + 40 pp.
adv.; consisting of Half-title, *Adrian Rome*, verso
blank; Title-page, as above, verso blank; Text, pp.

[1]—364; imprint at foot, *Printed by Morrison and Gibb Limited, Edinburgh*; 40 pp. advertisements, dated *February 1899*. Headlines throughout, *Adrian Rome.*

Signatures: two leaves, unsigned; 1—22, by eights; 23, six leaves; adv., [A], four leaves; A2, four; A3, eight; [A4], four leaves.

Issued in blue cloth lettered in gold on back, *Adrian / Rome / — / Ernest Dowson / & Arthur Moore /* [gilt ornamentation down to] */ Methuen*; on front cover, *Adrian Rome*, plus small gilt ornaments.

Published price, 6s.

(55)

[VOLTAIRE : La Pucelle : 1899]

La Pucelle The Maid of Orleans : / An Heroic-Comical Poem in Twenty- / One Cantos by Arouet de Voltaire : / A New and Complete Translation In- / To English Verse Revised Cor- / rected / and Augmented From the Earlier / English Translation of W. H. Ireland / and the One Attributed to Lady / Charleville with the Variants Now / For the First Time Translated By / Ernest Dowson : In Two Volumes : / Volume One [*Two*] / London : Printed for The / Lutetian Society 1899

Collation : 2 vols., Royal octavo, 8½ × 6¾.

Vol. One; pp. iv + 210; consisting of Half-title, *The Maid of Orleans,* verso notice of limitation of

edition; Title-page, as above, in red and black, verso
blank; Text, pp. [1]—209, verso blank.

Signatures: two leaves, unsigned; [1]—13, by
eights; 14, one leaf only.

Vol. Two; pp. iv + 211—408; consisting of preliminary leaves, as in Vol. One; Text, pp. 211—406;
2 pp. blank.

Signatures: nine leaves, unsigned; 15—25, by eights;
26, four leaves.

Issued in cream coloured cloth backed with blue linen,
lettered in gold on back, *La / Pucelle / (The / Maid /
of / Orleans) / By / Voltaire / Vol. I* [II] */ The /
Lutetian / Society / 1899.*

Published price, 42s.

The edition is limited to 500 numbered copies.

(56)

[MEMOIRS OF CARDINAL DUBOIS : 1899]

Memoirs / of / Cardinal Dubois / Translated
from the French / By Ernest Dowson / With
Photogravure Portraits / of Cardinal Dubois and
/ The Duc D'Orléans / [*Ornament*] / In Two
Volumes—Volume One [*Two*] / London /
Leonard Smithers and Co / 5 Old Bond Street W
/ 1899

Collation : 2 vols., Demy octavo, 8⅞ × 5⅝.

Volume One; pp. xvi + 284; consisting of 2 pp. blank;
Half-title, *Secret Memoirs of the / Court of France
/ During the / XVIIth and XVIIIth Centuries,*

verso blank; Frontispiece; Title-page, as above, in red and black; verso blank; *Contents*, pp. vii—xii; Prefatory Note, pp. xiii—xvi; Text, pp. [1]—282; imprint, *W. H. White and Co. Ltd., Riverside Press, Edinburgh*; pp. [283—4], blank. Headlines throughout : recto, chapter number; verso, *Memoirs of Cardinal Dubois.*
Signatures : 8 leaves, unsigned; A—R, by 8s; S, 4; T, 2 leaves.

Volume Two; pp. viii + 268; Half-title, Frontispiece, and Title-page, as in Vol. One; *Contents*, pp. [v]— viii; Text, pp. [1]—257, verso blank; Index pp. 259—268; imprint, as in Vol. I, at foot of page.

Issued in royal purple cloth lettered in gold on back, *Memoirs / of / Cardinal / Dubois / Vol. I* [II] / *Leonard / Smithers / and Co. / 1899*; Fleur-de-lys in gold on front cover.

Published price, 21s.

(57)

[DECORATIONS : 1899]

Decorations : / In Verse and Prose / By / Ernest Dowson / Leonard Smithers and Co/ 5 Old Bond Street / London W / MDCCCXCIX

Collation : Square octavo, $7\frac{1}{2}$ × $5\frac{3}{4}$; pp. xii + 52; consisting of Half-title *Decorations: / In Verse and Prose*, verso, *By the same author*; Title-page, as above, in red and black; verso, *Chiswick Press:— Charles Whittingham and Co. Tooks Court, Chancery Lane, London.*; Acknowledgment, verso blank;

Contents, pp. [vii]—viii; *Beyond*, verso blank; Fly-title, verso blank; Text, pp. [1]—50; p. [51], ornament and imprint; verso blank. There are 31 verse pieces and 5 prose.

Signatures : [A], 6 leaves; B—D, by 8s; E, 2 leaves.

Issued in cream coloured parchment boards lettered in gold on back, *Decor / ations / By / Ernest / Dowson / Leonard / Smithers / and Co / 1899*; on front cover, design in gold lettered in gold, *Decorations*; Design on back cover signed with initials in lower right hand corner.

Published price, 5s.

The front cover design is by Pickford Waller; the reverse cover, by Althea Giles. Beardsley had no hand in either, as is generally supposed.

The following poems are here reprinted : *The Three Witches* (*Savoy*, No. 6, Oct., 1896); *Saint Germain-en-Laye* (*Savoy*, No. 2, Apr., 1896); *In a Breton Cemetery* (*The Pageant*, 1896); *A Song* (*Savoy*, No. 5, Sept., 1896); *Breton Afternoon* (*Savoy*, No. 3, July, 1896); *Venite Descendamus* (*Savoy*, No. 4, Aug. 1896); *A Last Word* (*Savoy*, No. 7, 1896, under the title of *Epilogue*).

(58)

[POEMS : 1905]

The Poems of / Ernest Dowson / With a Memoir by / Arthur Symons / Four Illustrations by / Aubrey Beardsley / and a Portrait by / William Rothenstein / John Lane, The Bodley Head / London & New York MDCCCCV

Collation: Crown octavo, 7⅜ × 4¾; pp. 2 + xxxviii + 168; consisting of blank leaf; Half-title, *The Poems of / Ernest Dowson*, verso blank; Frontispiece; Title-page, as above, in red and black, verso, imprint, *Printed by Ballantyne, Hanson & Co. London & Edinburgh*; *Ernest Dowson* [Memoir], by Symons, pp. v—xxix, verso blank; *Contents*, pp. xxxi—xxxiv; *Illustrations*, p. xxxv, verso blank; *In Preface*, pp. xxxvii—xxxviii; Fly-title, p. [1]; Text, pp. 2—166; slip inserted (facing p. 166) bearing Acknowledgment of source of the Memoir; advertisements, pp. [167—8]. Headlines, when occurring, according to the text.

Signatures: [a] & b, by 8s; c, 4 leaves; A—K, by 8s; L, 4 leaves.

Issued in green cloth lettered in gold on back, *The / Poems / of / Ernest / Dowson / John Lane*; gold design on cover, signed in lower right hand corner; top edges gilt. Published price, 5s.

First Collected Edition: *Verses* are reprinted from the edition of *1896*; *The Pierrot of the Minute*, from that of *1897*; *Decorations* [1899]; the *Memoir*, by Symons, appeared originally in *Studies in Prose and Verse* [1904]. Beardsley's illustrations are from *The Pierrot of the Minute*.

(59)

[DE GONCOURT: Confidantes of a King: 1907]

The Confidantes / of a King / The Mistresses of Louis XV. / By E. De Goncourt / Translated by

/ Ernest Dowson / With Portraits / Vol. I [*II*]
/ T. N. Foulis / London and Edinburgh / 1907

Collation : 2 vols., Royal octavo, 8¾ × 5½.

Vol. I; pp. viii + 232; consisting of Half-title,
Confidantes / of a King, verso blank ; Frontispiece ;
Title-page, as above, verso blank ; *Illustrations,* verso
blank ; *Chapters,* verso blank ; Text, pp. [1]—232.
Headlines throughout : verso, *The Mistresses of
Louis XV.* ; recto, various.

Signatures : 4 leaves, unsigned ; A—O, by 8s ; P,
4 leaves.

Vol. II; pp. viii + 228; preliminary leaves, as in Vol.
I; Text, pp. [1]—225, verso blank ; pp. [227—8],
blank. Headlines, as in Vol. I.

Signatures : 4 leaves, unsigned ; IIA—IIO, by 8s ;
IIP, 2 leaves.

Issued in scarlet cloth, lettered in gold on back, *The /
Confid- / antes / of a / King / E. De / Goncourt /
Vol I* [II] */ T. N. Foulis*; blind tooled fleur-de-lys on
back, and on front cover; gold ornament in centre of
front cover. Scarlet end papers.

(60)

[BEAUTY & THE BEAST : 1908]

The Story of / Beauty & The Beast / The Com-
plete Fairy Story / Translated from the French
/ By Ernest Dowson [*Ornaments*] / With Four
Plates in Colour / By Charles Conder [*Orna-
ments*] / London : John Lane, The Bodley Head
/ New York : John Lane Company. MCMVIII

Collation : Quarto, 11¼ × 8¾; pp. x + 120; consisting of Half-title, *The Story of / Beauty & the Beast,* verso Advertisement; Frontispiece; Title-page, in red and black, as above, verso, *William Clowes & Sons, Limited, Printers, London*; p. [5], blank, verso, Notice of Limitation; *List of Plates,* verso blank; Fly-title, *The Story of / Beauty & the Beast,* verso blank; Text, pp. 1—119, verso blank. Head-lines throughout, *Beauty and the Beast.*

Signatures : [A], 5 leaves; B—Q, by 4s.

Issued in green cloth, ribbed, lettered in gold on back, *The / Story / of / Beauty / and the / Beast / Dowson / The / Bodley Head*; there is an ornament in gold on the front cover; top edge gilt. There was an orange dust wrapper.

Published price, 10s 6d.

The edition consisted of 300 copies of which 260 were for sale.

(61)

[PLARR : *Ernest Dowson* : 1914]

Ernest Dowson / 1888—1897 / Reminiscences, Unpublished Letters / and Marginalia / By / Victor Plarr / With a Bibliography compiled by / H. Guy Harrison / London / Elkin Mathews, Cork Street / M CM XIV

Collation : Crown octavo, 7 7/16 × 5; pp. 148; consisting of Half-title, *Ernest Dowson,* verso blank; Title-page, as above, verso blank; p. [5], quotation from Holbrook Jackson, verso blank; *Contents,* verso blank; *A Word of Explanation,* pp. 9—10;

Text, pp. 11—147; imprint at foot, *The Riverside Press Limited, Edinburgh*; p. [148], advertisements. Verso headlines throughout, *Ernest Dowson*; Chapter headings, recto.

Signatures : [A]—I, by 8s; K, 2 leaves.

Issued in red cloth lettered in gold, on back, *Ernest / Dowson / Victor / Plarr / Elkin / Mathews*, and on front cover, *Ernest Dowson / Victor Plarr.* White end papers.

Published price, 3s 6d.

A great many of Dowson's letters are here printed for the first time.

(62)

[ET CETERA : 1924]

Et Cetera / Pascal Covici / Chicago / 1924

The above volume (I quote the title-page from memory) contains a sonnet *Tennyson,* of Dowson's. The volume is a royal octavo, black cloth, gilt, and was published at $7.50. The edition was limited to 750 copies.

KATHERINE MANSFIELD
1888—1923

IN A GERMAN PENSION

BY

KATHERINE MANSFIELD

LONDON

STEPHEN SWIFT & CO. LTD

10 John Street, Adelphi

Facsimile, actual size of type, of Title-page of No. 63.

KATHERINE MANSFIELD

(63)

[IN A GERMAN PENSION : 1911]

In a German / Pension / By / Katherine Mansfield / [*Publisher's device*] / London / Stephen
Swift & Co. Ltd / 10 John Street, Adelphi

Collation : Crown octavo, 7⅝ × 4⅞; pp. 252 + 4 pp. adv.
+ 32 pp. adv.; consisting of a Half-title, *In a German
Pension*, verso blank; Title-page, as above, verso
blank; Contents, verso blank; Text, pp. 7—251;
verso, imprint, *The Riverside Press Limited,
Edinburgh.*; Advertisements, 4 pp. (numbered 1—4)
included in Sig. Q; 32 pp. advertisements, printed
in red and black; imprint *Neill and Co. Ltd.* at foot
of page 32. Headlines throughout: verso, *In a
German Pension*; recto, chapter headings. There
are 13 stories.

Signatures: [A]—Q, by 8s; + 16 leaves adv.,
unsigned.

Issued in green cloth lettered in gold on back, *In a /
German / Pension / Katherine / Mansfield* / [Ornament]
/ *Stephen / Swift*; on front cover (blind tooled with
design of arrows and books), *In a German / Pension /
Katherine Mansfield* in gold. There was an ochre dust
wrapper.

Published price, 6s.

(64)

[JE NE PARLE PAS FRANCAIS : 1919]

Je Ne Parle Pas Francais / By / Katherine Mansfield / [*Ornament*] / The Heron Press : Hampstead / MCMXIX

Collation : Quarto, 10⅛ × 7¾; pp. vi + 30; consisting of pp. [i—iv], blank; Title-page, as above, verso blank; Text, pp. 1—25, verso, Notice of Limitation; pp. [27—30], blank. There are no signatures.

Issued in green wrappers; there is a white paper label on front cover (4¼ × 1¹¹⁄₁₆) reading *Je Ne Parle Pas Francais / By Katherine Mansfield* within one line ruled border.

Published price, 10s 6d.

The edition consists of 100 copies.

(65)

[PRELUDE : 1920]

Prelude / By / Katherine Mansfield / Hogarth Press / Richmond.

Collation : quarto, 7⅞ × 5⅞; pp. 68; consisting of blank leaf, pp. [1]—[2] ; Title-page, as above, verso blank; p. [5] *To L.H.B. and J.M.M.*, verso, blank; Text, pp. [7]—68; imprint, *Printed by Leonard and Virginia Woolf at the Hogarth Press.* at foot of page 68. Headlines, recto and verso, *The Prelude*, to page 20; p. 21 and following, *Prelude*.

There are no signatures.

Issued in royal-blue wrappers lettered in black on front cover, *Prelude / Katherine Mansfield.* Wrappers measure 8½ × 6.

Published price, 3s 6d.

The edition consists of 250 copies.

(66)

[BLISS : 1920]

Bliss / And Other Stories / By Katherine / Mansfield / [*Sm. Printer's ornament*] / London : Constable / & Company Limited

Collation : Crown octavo, 6¼ × 4⅞; pp. viii + 280; consisting of Half-title, *Bliss / & Other / Stories / [Ornament]*, verso, "*. . . but I tell you, my lord fool, out of this nettle / danger, we pluck this flower, safety.*"; Title-page, as above, verso, *Published 1920*; p. [v], *To / John Middleton Murry*; verso blank; Contents, p. [vii], verso blank; Text, pp. 1—[280]; imprint at foot of page, *Printed in Great Britain at The Mayflower Press, Plymouth. William Brendon & Son, Ltd.* Headlines throughout according to chapter. Page 13, misnumbered " 3." There are 14 stories.

Signatures : [A], 4 leaves; B—S, by 8s; T, 4 leaves.

Issued in brick red cloth, lettered in black, on back, *Bliss / By / Katherine / Mansfield / Constable*; on front cover, within black ruled border, *Bliss / & Other Stories / By Katherine / Mansfield.* White end papers. There was a white dust wrapper with portrait of the author on front.

Published price, 9s.

The lettering on the cover should be in quite narrow characters. Some copies have thicker characters and the cloth shows the white weave beneath. Such copies are rebound.

(67)

[THE GARDEN PARTY: 1922]

The / Garden Party / and Other Stories / By Katherine / Mansfield / *Montaigne dit que les hommes vont béant / aux choses futures; j'ai la manie de béer / aux choses passées.* / London Bombay Sydney / Constable & Company Limited

Collation: Crown octavo, $7\frac{1}{2} \times 4\frac{7}{8}$; pp. 276; consisting of the Half-title, *The Garden Party / and Other Stories*; verso, bears notices of *Bliss*; Title-page, as above; verso, Dedication and notice, *First Published, 1922*; Contents, verso blank; Text, pp. 7—276; imprint, *Printed in Great Britain by Butler & Tanner, Frome and London* at foot of page. Headlines recto and verso with each section. There are 15 stories.

Signatures: [A]—Q by 8s; R, 2 leaves, enclosing R*, 8 leaves.

Issued in sky-blue cloth lettered in dark blue on back, *The · Garden / Party ¦· By / Katherine / Mansfield / Author · of / Bliss / Constable*; on front, in dark blue, *The · Garden / Party · and / Other ·: Stories / Katherine / Mansfield / Author · of / Bliss*; Panelling in blue on back and on front cover. There was a strawberry coloured dust wrapper.

Published price, 7s 6d.

There were 25 copies so issued, lettered in blue; the greater part was taken by travellers or sent to Australia, as this was merely a binders' trial issue. It was decided that the colour did not show well enough, and the lettering on the later issue of the First Edition was in ochre.

Misprint in first two issues; p. 103, last line, extra " s " inserted.

(68)

[THE DOVES' NEST: 1923]

The / Doves' Nest / And Other Stories / By Katherine / Mansfield / " *Reverence, that angel of the world* " / London Bombay Sydney / Constable & Company Limited

Collation: Crown octavo, $7\frac{1}{2} \times 4\frac{7}{8}$; pp. xxiv + 200; consisting of Half-title, *The Doves' Nest / and Other Stories*, verso, blank; Title-page, as above, verso bearing imprint at foot, *Printed in Great Britain by Robert Maclehose and Co., Ltd. The University Press, Glasgow*·; *To / Walter De La Mare*, verso blank; Contents, verso blank; *Introductory Note*, pp. ix—xxiii, verso blank; Text, pp. 1—[197]; imprint of Maclehose repeated at foot of page; pp. [198]—[200] blank. Headlines recto and verso with the story.

Signature [a], 4 leaves; b, 8 leaves; A—M, by 8s; N, 4 leaves.

Issued in blue-grey cloth lettered in blue on back *The · Doves' / Nest ·: By / Katherine / Mansfield / Constable*; and on front cover, *The · Doves' / Nest / Katherine / Mansfield*; panelling in blue on back and on front cover.   White end papers.   There was a grey dust wrapper.

Published price, 6s.

Twenty-five copies were sent out as travellers' samples, lacking the date on the back of the title.   The balance of the edition was issued with the addition of *First Published June, 1923* on the reverse of the title-page.

The letter " t " is missing from the first word line 8, p. 64, in the first two issues.

(69)

[POEMS : 1923]

Poems / By Katherine Mansfield / London : Constable & Co. Ltd.

Collation : quarto, 8⅜ × 6¾; pp. xii + 92 (including blank leaf); consisting of Half-title, *Poems*, verso, *By the same Author*; Title-page as above, verso, *First published 1923* at top of page, and at foot, *Printed in Great Britain by Robert Maclehose and Co. Ltd. The University Press, Glasgow*; Dedication; verso blank; Contents, pp. vii—ix, verso blank; Introductory Note, pp. xi—xii; Fly-title, *Poems 1909—1910*, verso blank; Text (with various Fly-titles), pp. 3—89; pp. [90—92], blank.   Poems headings at top of page; numbering at foot, centered. There are 69 poems.

Signatures : 6 unsigned leaves; A—K, by 4s; L, 2 leaves enclosing L2, 4 leaves.

Issued in brown boards, backed with tan cloth; red leather label on back lettered in gold, *Poems / Katherine*

/ *Mansfield.* At the foot, the cloth is stamped in gold, *1923.* There was a cream coloured dust wrapper.

Published price, 14s.

(70)

[SOMETHING CHILDISH: 1924]

Something / Childish / and Other Stories / By / Katherine / Mansfield / *A little bird was asked: Why are your / songs so short? He replied: I have many / songs to sing, and I should like to sing / them all.* / Anton Tchehov / Constable & Co. Ltd. / London

Collation: Crown octavo, $7\frac{3}{8} \times 4\frac{3}{4}$; pp. 2 + x + 260; consisting of blank leaf, included in the signature; Half-title, *Something Childish / and Other Stories*; verso, *By the Same Author*; Title-page as above; verso, imprint at foot, *Printed in Great Britain by Robert Maclehose and Co. Ltd. The University Press, Glasgow.*; Dedication, *To H. M. Tomlinson,* verso blank; Contents, verso blank; *Introductory Note*, pp. ix—[x]; Text, pp. 1—[259]; imprint repeated at foot of page; p. [260], blank. Headlines throughout are the same recto and verso, but vary with the story. There are 25 stories.

Signatures: 6 leaves unsigned; A—P, by 8s; Q, 2 leaves, encloses Q2, 8 leaves.

Issued in grey buckram lettered and panelled on back in dark blue, *Something / Childish / Katherine / Mansfield / Constable*; on front cover, *Something / Childish / & Other Stories / Katherine / Mansfield,* and panelling in blue.   There was a grey dust wrapper similar to the binding.

Published price, 6s.

Of this first issue, 34 copies escaped destruction; these were used as travellers' samples, sent to Australia, or given for early review.   The second issue bears the notice, *First published, 1924,* on reverse of title.

CONTRIBUTIONS TO

PERIODICAL LITERATURE

BY KATHERINE MANSFIELD

Katherine Mansfield has contributed to the following periodicals, some of which are extremely difficult to find :

New Age.

Rhythm. Nos. 1—4 were issued in grey wrappers, with design by J. D. Ferguson. Of No. 1, (Summer, 1911), there were two impressions of 250 copies each; of No. 2 (Autumn, 1911), an edition of 500 copies; Nos. 3 & 4, 750 copies each. Nos. 5—14 were published monthly from June 1912 until March 1913, in large editions, bound in bright blue wrappers.

Blue Review. Nos. 1—3, May—July, 1913, bound in bright blue wrappers printed with title and contents.

Signature. Nos. 1—3 (Oct. 4, Oct. 18, & Nov. 1, 1915), *Published by subscription only,* price 2/6 for six copies. Contains *Autumns,* etc. by Katherine Mansfield, under the pseudonym of *Matilda Berry.* Of this publication, 250 copies were printed; 120 were destroyed.

Athenæum, under the pseudonym of *Elizabeth Stanley.*
English Review.
London Mercury.
Adelphi.

There is some original poetry which appears as a translation from a Russian (imaginary) by the name of *Boris Petrovsky.*

ALICE MEYNELL
1850—1922

ALICE MEYNELL

PART I: BOOKS AND TRANSLATIONS

(71)

[PRELUDES : 1875]

Preludes. / By / A. C. Thompson. / With Illustrations and Ornaments by / Elizabeth Thompson. / [*ornament*] / Henry S. King & Co., / 65, Cornhill, and 12, Paternoster Row, London. / 1875.

Collation: Crown octavo, 7⅞ × 5½; pp. viii + 84; consisting of Half-title, *Preludes.*, verso bearing ornament; *Frontispiece*; Title-page, as above, verso bearing ornament; Dedication, *To My Father and Mother.*, verso, ornament; *Contents*, pp. [vii]—viii; *Author's Errata* slip (3 corrections); Text, pp. [1]—84; *Note* and imprint of *Unwin Brothers* at foot. Beside the Frontispiece, there are five full page illustrations. Headlines according to the text. There are 37 poems.

Signatures: [1], four leaves; 2—6, by eights; 7, two leaves.

Issued in green cloth gilt, lettered lengthwise on back, *Preludes A. C. Thompson*; five gilt ornaments on front cover. Chocolate end papers.

Published price, 7s 6d.

(72)

[SONNETS OF THREE CENTURIES : 1882]

Sonnets / of / Three Centuries : / A Selection / Including / Many Examples Hitherto Unpublished. / Edited by T. Hall Caine. / London : Elliot Stock, 62 Paternoster Row. / 1882.

Collation : Quarto, 8⅝ × 6¾; pp. xxxvi + 2 + 332.
   Renouncement, by Alice Meynell (p. 263) is first printed here.

Issued in blue cloth decorated in gold; lettered on back, *Sonnets / of Three / Centuries / Hall Caine.*

Published price, 15s.

   This sonnet was included at the suggestion of D. G. Rossetti, who had seen it in manuscript, and described it as one of the finest sonnets ever written by a woman.

(73)

[SOME MODERN ARTISTS : 1883]

Some Modern Artists / and Their Work. / Edited by / Wilfrid Meynell. / [*Ornament*] / Cassell & Company, Limited : / London, Paris & New York. / [All Rights Reserved.] / 1883.

Collation : Royal quarto, 10⅝ × 8½; pp. xii + 244 + 4 pp. adv.; consisting of Half-title; Frontispiece (reckoned in the pagination); Title-page, as above; *Contents,* pp. [vii]—viii; List of Illustrations, pp. [ix]—xi, verso blank; Text, pp. [1]—244; Advertisements, 4 pp.

Signatures: [A], 5 leaves; B—EE, by 4s; FF, 2 leaves.

Issued in green cloth embossed with floral designs; lettered in gold: on back, *Some / Modern / Artists / And Their / Work*; on front cover, *Some Modern / Artists / And Their Work*. Top edge gilt.

Published price, 12s 6d.

Mrs. Meynell has contributed *G. H. Boughton, A.R.A.,* pp. 21—31; and *Jean Louis Ernest Meissonier,* pp. 46 —51.

(74)

[THE POOR SISTERS OF NAZARETH : 1889]

The / Poor Sisters of Nazareth. / An Illustrated Record / of / Life at Nazareth House, Hammersmith. / Drawn by / George Lambert; / Written by / Alice Meynell; / Published by / Burns & Oates, Limited. / London : 28 Orchard Street, W., and 63 Paternoster Row, E.C. / And at New York.

Collation: Royal quarto, 12¼ × 9¾; pp. 2 + 48 + 2; consisting of blank leaf; p. [1], blank, verso, Frontispiece; Title-page, as above, verso blank; Dedication, verso blank; Text, pp. [7]—45, verso blank; *The Branch Houses . . .*, verso blank; blank leaf. Headlines throughout, *The Poor Sisters of Nazareth.* The book is printed throughout in brown.

Signatures: [A]—F, by 4s.

Issued in pictorial boards with white parchment back; lettered on front cover, *The Poor Sisters / of / Nazareth*

/ *Sketched* / *By* / *George* / *Lambert* / *Written* / *by* / *Alice Meynell* / *Burns & Oates* / *Limited* / *London* & / *New York.*

Published price, 2s 6d.

(75)

[THE RHYTHM OF LIFE: 1893]

The / Rhythm of Life / And Other Essays / By / Alice Meynell / [*Ornament*] / London / Elkin Mathews and / John Lane / 1893

Collation: *Small Paper Copy.* Post octavo, 6⅞ × 4⅜; pp. viii + 108 + 2 pp. adv.; consisting of Half-title, *The Rhythm of Life / And Other Essays*, verso, *By the same Author*; Title-page, as above, verso, Notice of Limitation; Contents, verso blank; Fly-title, *The Rhythm of Life*, verso blank; Text, pp. [1]—106; imprint at foot, *Printed by T. and A. Constable, Printers to Her Majesty, at the Edinburgh University Press.*; Notice of Indebtedness, p. [107], verso blank; 2 pp. advertisements inserted. Head-lines throughout, various. There are 20 essays.

Signatures: 4 leaves, unsigned; A—F, by 8s; G, 4, H, 2 leaves.

Edition consists of 500 copies.

Collation: *Large Paper Copy.* Demy octavo, 9 ×5⅝; pp. x + 108 + 2; collation follows that of the small paper copies, with the exception that the Notice of Limitation is signed by the Authoress, and that p. x has the Notice of Indebtedness.

Edition consists of 50 copies.

Issued in tan buckram lettered in gold: on back, *The /
Rhythm / of / Life / Alice Meynell / Elkin Mathews
/ and / John Lane*; on front cover, *The Rhythm of Life
/ Alice Meynell.*

Published price, small paper edition, 5s.

(76)

[POEMS : 1893]

Poems / By / Alice Meynell / [*Ornament*] /
London / Elkin Mathews and / John Lane / 1893

Collation: *Small Paper Copy.* Post octavo, 6⅞ × 4⅜;
pp. xii + 76; consisting of Half-title, *Poems by
Alice Meynell*, verso, *By the same Author*; Title-
page, as above, verso Notice of Limitation; Dedication, verso blank; Contents, pp. [vii]—ix, verso
blank; Fly-title, *Poems*, verso blank; Text, pp. [1]
—72; Notice of Sources, verso, *Printed by T. and
A. Constable, Printers to Her Majesty, at the Edinburgh University Press.*; Advertisements, pp. [75—
6]. Headlines throughout, various. There are 39
Poems.

Signatures: [a], 2; a2, 4 leaves; A—D, by 8s; E,
4; F, 2 leaves.

The edition consists of 550 copies.

Collation: Large Paper Copy. Demy octavo, 9 × 5⅝;
collation similar to the small paper edition; the
Notice of Limitation on the reverse of title is signed
by the authoress.

The edition consists of 50 copies.

G

Issued in tan buckram lettered in gold: on back, *Poems / Alice / Meynell / Elkin Mathews / and / John Lane*; on front cover, *Poems / Alice Meynell*.

Published price, small paper copies, 3s 6d.

Many of the Verses are reprinted from *Preludes*.

(77)

[WILLIAM HOLMAN HUNT: 1893]

The Art Annual / - / William Holman Hunt / His Life and Work / By / W. Farrar, D.D., F.R.S. / Archdeacon and Canon of Westminster / and / Mrs. Meynell / With numerous illustrations / [*Ornament*] / London: Art Journal Office, 26, Ivy Lane, Paternoster Row / 1893

Collation: Folio, 13 × 9⅞; pp. 4 + 32 + 16 pp. adv.; consisting of Half-title, *William Holman Hunt / His Life and Work*, verso blank; Frontispiece; Title-page, as above, verso blank; Text, pp. [1] —32; 16 pp. advertisements. Headlines throughout.

Signatures: [A]—I, by 8s; + 8 leaves, adv.

Issued in decorated blue-green cloth; lettered in gold on front cover, *The / Life & Work / of / W. Holman Hunt / By / Archdeacon Farrar / and / Mrs. Meynell*; top edges gilt. Floreated end papers. Also issued in light brown wrappers as the *Xmas Number of the Art Journal*.

Published price; cloth, 5s; wrappers, 1s 6d.

(78)

[LOURDES : 1894]

Lourdes : Yester- / Day, To-Day, and / To-Mor-row. / By / Daniel Barbé. / Translated by / Alice Meynell. / ===== / *With Twelve Water-colour Drawings by Hoffbauer, reproduced / in Colours.* / ===== / London : Burns & Oates, Limited. / 28 Orchard Street, W.

Collation : Royal octavo, 10⅛ × 6½; pp. iv + 108 + 12 illustrations on glossed paper; consisting of Frontis-piece with tissue guard; Title-page, as above; verso, *Burns and Oates, Ld., Printers, London, W.*; *Table of Contents* and *of Illustrations*, verso blank; Fly-title, *Lourdes.*, verso blank; Text, pp. [3]—106 (including Fly-titles of each section); pp. [107]—[108], blank. The illustrations (pagination not given in Contents), occur as follows : frontis., pp. 6, 16, 22, 32, 38, 48, [64], 70, 80, and [96]. Chapter headings throughout, alike recto and verso.

Signatures : " [1] ", two leaves; " 2 "—" 7 ", by eights; " 8 ", four leaves; " 9 ", two leaves.

Issued in blue buckram lettered in gold, on back, *Lourdes / Burns & Oates*; on front, *Lourdes : / Yesterday, To-Day / To-Morrow / Translated by / Alice Meynell.* Top edges gilt.

Published price, 6s.

(79)

[OTHER POEMS : 1896]

Other Poems / By / Alice Meynell / [*Ornament*] / *Privately printed at the New Year, / 1896.*

Collation: Foolscap octavo, 6¼ × 4⅜; pp. 16; consisting
of Title-page, as above, verso blank; *To A.* [gnes]
T. [obin], verso blank; *Contents,* verso blank; Text,
pp. [7]—16.

Issued in white wrappers, lettered in orange on front
cover, *Other Poems / By / Alice Meynell /* [ornament].

Fifty copies were sent as Christmas Cards.

(80)

[THE COLOUR OF LIFE: 1896.]

The / Colour of Life / And Other Essays / On
Things Seen and Heard / By / Alice Meynell /
[*Ornament*] / John Lane: Vigo St. / Way and
Williams / Chicago / 1896

Collation: Post octavo, 6⅞ × 4⅜; pp. viii + 104 + 2 + 2
+ 16 pp. adv.; consisting of Half-title, *The Colour
of Life / And Other Essays / On Things Seen
And Heard*; verso, *Uniform with this*; Title-page,
as above, verso blank; Dedication, verso blank;
Contents, verso blank; Text, pp. [1]—103; verso,
below ornament, *Printed by W. H. White and Co.
Ltd. Edinburgh Riverside Press*; *By the Same
Author,* pp. [1]—2, and [1]—2; Advertisements,
16 numbered pages, dated *1896.* Headlines throughout, varying. There are 14 essays.

Signatures: 4 leaves, unsigned; A—F, by 8s; G, 4;
H, 2 leaves; plus 8 leaves adv.

Issued in red buckram lettered in gold on back, *The /
Colour / of / Life / Alice / Meynell / The / Bodley
/ Head / and / Chicago.*

Published price, 3s 6d.

(81)

[The Children : 1897]

The / Children / By Alice Meynell / [*Cut*] / 1897 / John Lane / The / Bodley Head / London / & New York

Collation : Foolscap octavo, 6⅞ × 4¼; pp. 96 + 4 pp. adv. + 12 pp. adv.; consisting of Half-title, *The Children*, verso, *By the Same Author* (tissue guard to title-page); Title-page, as above, with figure of a child within ornamental border; verso, *Copyrighted in the United States / All rights reserved*; *To Their Best Friends*, verso blank; Contents, p. [7], verso blank; Text, pp. [9]—96; imprint at foot, *Printed by Pettitt & Cox, 23, Frith Street, Soho, London, W.*; 4 pp. advertisements, numbered; *List of Books For and About Children*, 12 pages, numbered; the last page is dated, *1896*. Headlines throughout, recto and verso, the chapter heading. There are 18 essays.

Signatures : [A], 4 leaves; B—F, by 8s; G, 4 leaves. The advertisements are not signed.

Issued in blue buckram, gilt, lettered in gold on back, *The / Child / Ren / Alice / Meynell / John / Lane / The / Bodley / Head*; on front, *The Children / By / Alice / Meynell*. There are ornaments in gold on back and on the front cover; on front cover, figure of a child in gold. White end papers.

Published price, 3s 6d.

(82)

[LONDON IMPRESSIONS : 1898]

London / Impressions / Etchings and Pictures / in Photogravure by / William Hyde / and Essays by / Alice Meynell / [*Photogravure*] / Westminster / Archibald Constable and Co. / 2 Whitehall Gardens / 1898

Collation : *Ordinary Issue*; Folio, 15½ × 11¼; pp. viii + 32; consisting of Half-title, *London Impressions*, verso blank; Title-page, as above, in red and black, verso blank; *List of Pictures*, pp. v—vi; *List of Essays*, pp. vii, verso blank; Text, pp. [1]—31, imprint below etching, *Edinburgh: T. and A. Constable, Printers to Her Majesty*; verso blank. Headlines throughout, *London Impressions*, verso; recto, chapter headings. Illustrations as per List. There are ten essays. There is a blank leaf of imitation parchment, front and back, tacked on to the end papers. The text is printed on *Unbleached Arnold* paper, watermarked, *1898*. Etching, *The River*, faces p. [1], instead of title, as listed.

Signatures : 4 leaves, unsigned; A—H, by 2s.

Issued in white parchment lettered lengthwise in gold on back, *London Impressions*; on front cover, in gold, *London / Impressions / Etchings and Pictures / in Photogravure by / William Hyde / and Essays by / Alice Meynell*.　Marbled end papers.

Published price, £8 8s.

Collation: *Large Paper Issue*; pp. 4 + viii + 32 + 4;
  consisting of blank leaf; p. [3], blank, verso Notice;
  balance of collation follows ordinary issue, with the
  addition of 4 blank pages at the end.   Printed
  throughout on Japanese Vellum and signed by the
  artist.

Issued in orange brown crush levant, gilt; lettered in
gold on back, *London / Impressions*, lengthwise, with
ornament; ornaments and ruling in gold on front and
back covers. Orange silk doublure; top edge gilt.

This special issue was limited to 15 copies.

(83)

[THE SPIRIT OF PLACE: 1899]

The Spirit of Place / And Other Essays / By /
Alice Meynell / [*Ornament*] / John Lane / The
Bodley Head / London and New York / 1899

Collation: Post octavo, 6⅝ × 4¼; pp. xii + 112 + 4;
  consisting of 4 pp. blank; Half-title, *The Spirit of
  Place / And Other Essays*; verso, *By the Same
  Author*; Title-page, as above; verso, *Copyright,
  1898, By John Lane* and imprint of *J. J. Little &
  Co Astor Place New York* within ornament;
  Dedication, verso blank; *Contents*, verso blank; Text,
  pp. [1]—106; *Advertisements*, pp. [107—110]; pp.
  [111-2], blank; 4 pp. blank. Headlines throughout
  according to the text. There are 17 essays.

  Signatures: six leaves, unsigned; 1—6, by eights;
  [7], ten leaves.

Issued in blue buckram lettered in gold: on back, *The / Spirit / of / Place / Alice / Meynell / The / Bodley / Head*; on front cover, *The Spirit of Place / Alice Meynell.*   Published price, 3s 6d.

(84)

[VENTURI : The Madonna : 1901]

The Madonna: / a Pictorial Representation of the Life and / Death of the Mother of Our Lord Jesus / Christ by the Painters and Sculptors of / Christendom in more than 500 of / Their Works / The Text translated from the Italian of / Adolfo Venturi with an Introduction by / Alice Meynell / Burns & Oates, Ltd., 28 Orchard St., London, W.

Collation: Royal quarto, 11¾ × 9¾; pp. 2 + xvi + 446 + 6; consisting of blank leaf; Half-title, *The Madonna,* verso blank; Frontispiece, with tissue guard; Title-page, as above, in red and black; verso, *Printed by Ballantyne, Hanson & Co. At the Ballantyne Press*; *Introduction,* pp. [v]—xiii, verso blank; *Contents,* verso blank; Text, pp. [1]—446; imprint of Ballantyne, Hanson, at foot; 3 blank leaves. Headlines throughout : *Introduction* to page xiii; thence, *The Madonna,* verso; recto, various.

Issued in blue buckram lettered in gilt on back, *The Ma- / - donna / Burns and Oates*; on front cover; *The Madonna.* There was a sky-blue dust wrapper.

Published price, 31s 6d.

The translation as well as the introduction is by Mrs. Meynell.

(85)

[LATER POEMS : 1902]

Later Poems / By Alice Meynell / Author of
" Poems " / [*Ornament*] / London and New
York / John Láne, The Bodley Head / 1902

Collation : Post octavo, 6⅞ × 4⅜; pp. iv + 44; consisting
of 2 blank leaves; Half-title, *Later Poems*, verso
blank; Title-page, as above, verso, *Copyright, 1901
By John Lane All rights reserved* and at foot, under
line, *University Press. John Wilson and Son.
Cambridge, U.S.A.*; Dedication, verso blank; Contents, pp. 7—8; Text, pp. 9—37, verso blank;
Advertisements, pp. [39—42]; pp. [43—4], blank.
Headlines throughout : verso, *Later Poems*; recto,
various. There are 19 poems.

Signatures : [1], eight leaves; 2, (pp. 13—28), eight
leaves, signed on p. 17; 3, eight leaves, signed on
p. 33.

Issued in blue cloth lettered in gold on back *Later /
Poems / Alice / Meynell / John / Lane*; gold floral
ornamentation on front cover, within double ruled border;
an inset is lettered *Later / Poems* [ornament].

Published price, 2s 6d.

Reprinted in *Collected Poems* (*1913*) and again under
the title of *The Shepherdess and Other Poems* (*1914,
etc.*). The latter contains no new poems (omits *Cradle-
Song at Twilight* and *A Poet's Wife* which are included
here) but contains the charming frontispiece, *Alice
Meynell. From an early sketch by Adrian Stokes, A.R.A.*

(86)

[CHILDREN OF OLD MASTERS : 1903]

Children / of the / Old Masters / (Italian School) / By / Alice Meynell / [*ornament*] / London / Duckworth and Co. / 3, Henrietta Street / Covent Garden, W.C. / 1903

Collation : Quarto, 12 × 9⅝; pp. x + 88; consisting of Half-title, *Children / of the / Old Masters*, verso, *All rights reserved.*; Frontispiece; Title-page, as above, in red and black, verso *Chiswick Press: Charles Whittingham and Co. Tooks Court, Chancery Lane, London.*; *To the Playmates*, verso blank; *Contents*, verso blank; *List of Illustrations*, pp. [ix—x] ; Text, pp. [1]—86; pp. [87], Ornament and Imprint; verso blank.

Signatures : [a], 4 leaves; b, 1 leaf; B—M, by 4s.

Issued in blue buckram lettered in gold : on back, *Children / of the / Old / Masters / Alice / Meynell / Duckworth & Co.*; on front cover, *Children / of the / Old Masters / Italian School /* [Ornament] / *Alice Meynell*, enclosed within gilt border. Top edge gilt.

Published price, 42s.

(87)

[THE QUEEN'S CAROL : 1905]

The Queen's / Carol / An Anthology of / Poems, Stories, Essays, Drawings / And Music by British Authors, / Artists and Composers / Published by the " Daily Mail ": / London, Manchester & Paris 1905

Collation: Quarto, 11⅛ × 8¾; pp. viii + 120; contains *The Watershed*, pp. 33—4, a poem by Alice Meynell, here for the first time published.

Issued in white cloth, lettered in green on back and on front cover.

(88)

[BAZIN : The Nun : 1908]

The Nun / By René Bazin / *Translated for the 25th French Edition / By A.M.* / London / Eveleigh Nash / 1908

Collation: Crown octavo, 7⅜ × 5; pp. viii + 256; consisting of (Frontispiece); Title-page, as above, verso blank; *Contents*, verso blank; Preface, pp. [v]—viii; Text, pp. [1]—254; *Printed by The Westminster Press (Gerrards, Ltd.) 11a, Harrow Road, W.*, verso blank.

Signatures: [1], four leaves; 2—17, by eights.

Issues in plum coloured cloth lettered in gold on back, *The / Nun / By / René / Bazin.*

Published price, 6s.

(89)

[CERES' RUNAWAY : 1909]

Ceres' Runaway / & Other Essays / By / Alice Meynell / London / Constable & Co, Ltd/ MCMIX

Collation: Crown octavo, 7⅜ × 4⅛; pp. 148; consisting of Half-title, *Ceres' Runaway / & Other Essays,* verso blank; Title-page, as above, verso blank; Contents, verso blank; Text, pp. 9—143, verso blank; Advertisements, pp. [145—6]; p. [147], blank, verso, *Letchworth: At the Arden Press.* Headlines throughout, varying. There are twenty-one essays.

Signatures: A—I, by 8s; I3, 2 leaves.

Issued in blue buckram lettered in gold: on back, *Ceres' / Run- / away / [Ornament] / By / Alice / Meynell*; on front cover, *Ceres' Runaway / And Other Essays / By / Alice Meynell* within one line gold border; gold lines at top and foot of back cover; top edge gilt.

A second issue of the first edition bears a cancel title-page with a double imprint ranged parallel:*Burns & Oates / 28 Orchard St / London / W.* and *Constable & Co / 10 Orange Street / London / W.C.*

(90)

[MARY, THE MOTHER OF JESUS: 1912]

Mary, The Mother / of Jesus: an Essay / By Alice Meynell. Illustrated / By R. Anning Bell, R.W.S. / [*ornament in blue*] / Philip Lee Warner, Publisher / To the Medici Society, W. MDCCCXII

Collation: Quarto, $11\frac{3}{4} \times 9\frac{1}{8}$; pp. 4 + viii + 144; consisting of pp. [1]—[3] blank, verso Notice of Limitation; Half-title *Mary, The Mother / of Jesus,* verso blank; Frontispiece; Title-page as above, verso blank; *Contents,* verso blank; *Illustrations,* verso blank; Text, including Fly-titles, pp. [1]—143, verso imprint *Printed at The Chiswick Press: Charles Whittingham and Co. Tooks Court, Chancery Lane, London. The Coloured Plates Engraved and Printed By Henry Stone and Son, Ltd. Banbury.* Headlines throughout, varying with Text.

Signatures : 2 leaves unsigned, [A]—I, by 4s.

Issued in vellum, lettered in gold on the back, *Mary / The Mother / of Jesus / Alice Meynell / Lee Warner*; gold decoration in lower right hand corner of front cover. Decorated end papers.

Price, £2 2s.

Edition limited to 250 copies· There was also a small paper edition (10½ × 7¾), price 16s.

(91)

[POEMS : 1913]

Poems / by / Alice Meynell / Burns & Oates / 28 Orchard Street / London W / 1913

Collation: *Small paper edition*; Quarto, 7⅝ × 5⅝; pp. 4 + 124 (including adv., etc.); consisting of 2 blank leaves; Half-title, *Collected Poems / Of Alice Meynell*, verso blank; Frontispiece; Title-page, as above, verso blank; *To W.M.*, verso blank; *The Contents*, pp. 7—9; Notice of Sources, verso; Fly-title, *Early Poems*, verso blank; Text, including following fly-titles, pp. 13—117, verso, *Printed in England at the Arden Press*; Advertisements, pp. [119—120]; pp. [121—4], blank.

Signatures: 2 leaves unsigned; [A]—P, by 4s; 2 leaves, unsigned.

Issued in blue buckram lettered in gold : on back, *Poems / By / Alice / Meynell /* [Ornament] */ The / Collected / Edition*; on front cover, *Poems / By / Alice Meynell*; gold tooled lines on back and on front cover.

Published price, 5s.

Collation: *Large Paper Edition*; Quarto, 8⅛ × 6; the collation agrees with the small paper copy, with the addition of a notice of limitation.

Issued in blue boards backed in buckram; a paper label reads, ——— */ Poems / by Alice / Meynell /*———.

The edition consists of 250 copies.

Published price, 10s 6d.

There is a post octavo edition published in the same year, differing from the ordinary edition only in size. This was, however, issued later than the above and was intended primarily for American circulation.

The small paper edition antedates the large paper (by two months.)

The Ninth Edition of this work adds some new poems.

(92)

[EVERARD MEYNELL : Life of Thompson : 1913]

The Life of / Francis Thompson / By Everard Meynell / Burns & Oates Ltd / 28 Orchard Street / London W / 1913.

Collation: Demy octavo; 8¾ × 5½; pp. 4 + xii + 364 + 4, consisting of 4 blank pages; Half-title, *The*

Life of / Francis Thompson, verso blank; Frontispiece; Title-page, as above, in red and black, verso
blank; *To Grazia,* verso blank; Acknowledgment,
verso blank; *Contents,* verso blank; *Illustrations,*
verso blank; Text, pp. [1]—361, imprint at foot
*Printed by Ballantyne, Hanson & Co. at Paul's
Work, Edinburgh;* pp. [362—4], blank; 4 blank
pages. Various headlines throughout.

Signatures: 2 leaves, unsigned; [a], 6 leaves; A—Y,
by 8s; Z, 6 leaves; 2 leaves, unsigned.

Issued in tan buckram lettered in gold; on back *The
Life / of / Francis / Thompson / Burns & / Oates
Ltd.;* on front cover, *The Life of / Francis Thompson /*
[Ornament] / *Everard Meynell.*

Published price, 15s.

Letters and articles by Alice Meynell are here for the
first time published.

(93)

[CHILDHOOD: 1913]

Childhood / By / Alice Meynell / [*Ornament*] /
Published by B. J. Batsford. London

Collation: Post octavo, $6\frac{1}{8} \times 4\frac{3}{4}$; pp. ii + 66; consisting
of Half-title, *Fellowship Books / Edited by Mary
Stratton / Childhood,* verso Title-page, as above,
within ruled borders; Text, pp. 1—[65], verso
Printed at the Ballantyne Press London 1913. There
are 11 essays.

Signatures: [A]—D, by 8s; E, 2 leaves.

Issued in blue cloth lettered in gold on back within one line ruled border, *Child- / hood /* [Ornament] / *Alice / Meynell /* [Ornamentation] / *Batsford*; there is a small ornament on the back cover; white end papers with ornamental black border; top edge gilt; dark blue ribbon book-mark. There was a white dust wrapper.

Published price, 2s.

(94)

[ESSAYS : 1914]

Essays / by / Alice Meynell / Burns & Oates / 28 Orchard Street / London, W. / 1914

Collation : *Small Paper*; Square octavo, $7\frac{3}{8} \times 5\frac{1}{4}$; pp. 2 + viii + 268 + vi; consisting of blank leaf; Half-title, *The Essays of / Alice Meynell*, verso blank; Etched frontispiece; Title-page, as above, verso *Chiswick Press: Charles Whittingham and Co. Tooks Court, Chancery Lane, London*; Contents, pp. v—vii, verso Notice of Sources; Text, including Fly-titles, pp. [1] —267, verso printer's ornament and imprint; Advertisements, pp. [i—iv] ; pp. [v—vi], blank. Headlines throughout, varying. There are 51 essays.

Signatures : [A], 4 leaves; B—R, by 8s; S, 6 leaves.

Issued in blue buckram lettered in gold : on back, *Essays* / [Ornament] / *Alice / Meynell*; on the front cover, *Essays* / [Ornament] / *Alice / Meynell*; top edge gilt. There was a green dust wrapper.

Published price, 5s.

Collation: *Large Paper*; Demy octavo, 8 × 5½; pp.
4 + viii + 268 + 2; consisting of 2 blank leaves;
collation follows the small paper copy to pp. [268];
+ 1 blank leaf. Notice of Limitation is on reverse
of Half-title.

Issued in blue boards backed with tan linen; paper label
on back reading [Double rule] */ Essays / by Alice /
Meynell /* [Double rule].

Of this edition on hand made paper there were 250
copies.

Published price, 10s 6d.

Most of these Essays were collected from the volumes
entitled *The Rhythm of Life, The Colour of Life, The
Spirit of Place, The Children,* and *Ceres' Runaway*; in
addition are *The Seventeenth Century, Prue, Mrs.
Johnson,* and *Madam Rolland,* here for the first time
published.

(95)

[THE SHEPHERDESS : 1914]

Reprint of *Later Poems* (1902). See note there-
under.

(96)

[TEN POEMS : 1915]

Ten Poems / By Alice Meynell / 1913-1915 /
[*Ornament*] / Westminster / The Romney Street
Press / 1915

H

Collation : Square octavo, 9 × 6⅞; pp. 16; consisting of Title-page, as above, verso Dedication; Text, pp. 3—15; verso Notice of Limitation.

Signatures : 8 leaves, sewn in the middle.

Issued in full limp vellum and with Italian coloured paper wrappers. There is no lettering on the binding.

Published price : vellum, £1 11s 6d; paper, £1 5s.

The edition consists of 50 copies.

(97)

[MERCIER : Pastoral Letter : 1915]

Pastoral Letter / Of His Eminence Cardinal / Mercier / Archbishop of Malines / Primate of Belgium / Christmas 1914 / [*Ornament*] / *Official Translation. All Rights reserved* / Burns & Oates Ltd. / 28 Orchard Street, London, W.

Collation : Demy octavo, 9 × 5¾; pp. 32; consisting of Frontispiece; Text, pp. 1—[32] ; imprint at foot, *Chiswick Press: Printed by C. T. Jacobi, Tooks Court, Chancery Lane, E.C.*

Signatures : A, 8 leaves; A2, 8 leaves, superimposed.

Issued in imitation parchment wrappers lettered on front cover as above, in red and black. Ornament on back cover.

The translation is by Alice Meynell.

(98)

[POEMS ON THE WAR : 1916]

Poems on / The War / By / Alice Meynell

Collation : Quarto, 9⅛ × 8⅞; pp. 8, consisting of Title-
page as above, within ruled border, verso blank;
Text, pp. [3—6] ; *Facsimile;* verso, Notice. There
are two poems.

No signatures.

Issued in stiff green wrappers; on the front cover is
reproduced the title-page.

Of this edition, 20 copies were printed for private
circulation by Clement Shorter.

(99)

[A FATHER OF WOMEN : 1917]

A Father of Women / and Other Poems / By /
Alice Meynell / Burns & Oates Ltd / 28 Orchard
Street / London W / 1917.

Collation : Crown octavo, 7⅞ × 5½; pp. 32; consisting
of Half-title, *The Father of Women / and Other
Poems,* verso blank; Title-page, as above, verso,
To V.L.; Contents, verso blank; Text, pp. 7—30; p.
[31], *Printed in England by W. H. Smith & Son,*
etc.; verso, advertisements. There are sixteen
poems. There are no signatures.

Issued in powder blue wrappers, 8 × 5¾, reproducing the
title-page, with the addition of *Price Two Shillings net.*
at foot.

Published price, 2s.

(100)

[HEARTS OF CONTROVERSY: 1917]

Hearts of / Controversy / By / Alice Meynell / Burns & Oates / 28 Orchard Street / London / W

Collation : Crown octavo, 7½ × 5; viii + 120; consisting of Half-title *"Hearts of Controversy"* / *Julius Cæsar*, verso blank; Title-page as above within border, verso blank; *The Contents*, verso blank; *Introduction*; verso blank; Text pp. 1—115, verso bears imprint *The Pelican* / [ornament in red and black] / *Press* / *Gough Square* / *Fleet Street* / *E.C.4* / *A branch of the Victoria* / *House Printing Co., Ltd.* / *21 Tudor Street* / *Fleet Street* / *E.C.4*; pp. [117]—[120] bear advertisements. Headlines throughout : verso *Hearts of Controversy*; recto varying. There are six essays.

Signatures [A]—I by 8s.

Issued in blue buckram lettered in gold on the back *Hearts* / *of* / *Controversy* / *By* / *Alice* / *Meynell*; on the front *Hearts of* / *Controversy* / *By* / *Alice Meynell.* White end papers. Top edges gilt. There was a blue dust wrapper.

Published price, 5s.

(101)

[VASSALL-PHILLIPS : Mother of Christ : 1920]

The Mother of / Christ; or, The / Blessed Virgin Mary / In Catholic Tradition, Theo-/ Logy, and

Devotion [*Ornaments*] / By O. R. Vassall-
Phillips, C.SS.R. / *Author of " The Mustard
Tree," " Catholic Christianity," " The Work of /
St. Optatus Translated into English."* / *Domine,
dilexi decorum Domus Tuae, et locum / habita-
tionis Gloriae Tuae.* / London / Burns Oates &
Washbourne Ltd. / 28 Orchard St., W.1. 8-10
Paternoster Row, E.C. / and at Manchester ·
Birmingham · and Glasgow / 1920

Collation: Crown octavo, 7¼ × 4¾; pp. xxviii + 524;
on the reverse of the Half-title is *Aenigma Christi*,
by Alice Meynell, written especially for this book,
appears in no other edition or collection.

Issued in purple cloth lettered on back in gold, *The /
Mother / of / Christ / Vassall-Phillips / Burns Oates
& / Washbourne.*

(102)

[SECOND PERSON SINGULAR: 1921]

The Second Person / Singular / And Other
Essays / By / Alice Meynell / Humphrey Milford
/ Oxford University Press / London Edinburgh
Glasgow Copenhagen / New York Toronto Mel-
bourne Cape Town / Bombay Calcutta Madras
Shanghai Peking / 1921

Collation: Crown octavo, 7⅝ × 5⅛; pp. 144; consisting
of Title-page, as above, verso blank; *To Celia Clark*,
verso blank; *Contents*, verso, Notice of Selection;
Text, pp. [7]—140; an errata slip of one line is
inserted facing p. 140; p. [141], *Printed in England*

at the Oxford University Press by Frederick Hall; verso, advertisements, pp. [143—4], blank. Headlines throughout according to the chapter. There are twenty essays. A duplicate label is inserted after p. [144].

Signatures: [A]—I, by 8s.

Issued in blue buckram with paper label on back; *The / Second / Person / Singular / Alice Meynell / Milford.*

Published price, 6s.

(103)

[LAST POEMS: 1923]

The Last Poems of / Alice Meynell / [*asterisks*] / Burns, Oates and Washbourne Ltd. / 28 Orchard Street, W.1 / 8-10 Paternoster Row, E.C.4 / London / 1923

Collation: Post octavo, $7\frac{1}{2} \times 5\frac{1}{8}$; pp. 4 + 58; consisting of a blank leaf; Half-title, *The Last Poems / of Alice Meynell*, verso blank; Title-page, as above, within ornamental border; verso blank; *The Contents*, pp. [3—4]; pp. [5—6], blank; Text, pp. 7—54; pp. [55], blank; Advertisements, pp. [56—7]; verso Ornament and *At the Pelican Press.*

There are no Signatures.

Issued in brown boards; paper label on back reads ****** / *Last / Poems / of / Alice / Meynell / ******

Published price, 3s 6d.

(104)

[THE POEMS OF: 1923]

The Poems of / Alice Meynell / [*asterisk*] / Complete Edition / [*asterisk*] / Burns Oates & Washbourne Ltd / 28 Orchard Street WI / 8-10 Paternoster Row E.C.4 / London / 1923

Collation : Large Paper Edition; Demy octavo, $9\frac{1}{8} \times 5\frac{1}{2}$; pp. x + 146; consisting of Half-title, *The Poems of / Alice Meynell* / [asterisk] / *Complete Edition*; verso Notice of Limitation; Frontispiece (from the Edition of 1913); Title-page, as above, verso *Made and Printed in Great Britain*; *To W. M.*, verso, *Bibliographical Note*; *The Contents*, pp. vii—x; Text, including Fly-titles, pp. 1—144; pp. [145—6], blank. There is the portrait (from *School of Poetry*) facing p. 115.

Signatures : [A], 2 leaves; B, 6 leaves; C, 2; D, 6; E, 2; F, 6; G, 2; H, 6; I, 2; K, 6; L, 2; M, 6; N, 2; O, 6; P, 2; Q, 6; R, 2; S, 6; T, 2; U, 4 leaves.

Issued in blue buckram lettered in gold : on back, *Poems / of / Alice / Meynell* / [Asterisk] / *Complete / Edition*; on front cover, *The Poems of / Alice Meynell* / [Asterisk] / *Complete Edition.* Top edges gilt.

Published price, 18s.

PART II:

BOOKS WITH AN INTRODUCTION
BY ALICE MEYNELL

(105)

[LANGLEY: Fisher-Life: 1893]

Exhibition No. 103. / - / Catalogue / of a / Collection of / Water-Colour Drawings / Illustrating / Fisher-Life / With a Prefatory Note / By / Mrs. Meynell / Exhibited at / The Fine Art Society's. / 148, New Bond Street, / London. / *February,* 1893.

Collation: Crown octavo, $8\frac{3}{8} \times 5\frac{3}{8}$; pp. 2 + 12 + 2; consisting of 2 pp. advertisements; Title-page, as above, verso blank; *Prefatory Note* by Mrs Meynell, pp. [3]—7; etc.

Issued in grey wrappers; on front cover is reproduced the title-page (lacking comma after 148, in the third line from the end); advertisements on back and inside wrappers.

(106)

[HAKE: POEMS: 1894]

The Poems of / Thomas Gordon Hake / Selected / With a Prefatory Note by / Alice Meynell /

And a Portrait by / Dante Gabriel / Rossetti / London : Elkin Mathews and / John Lane / Chicago : Stone and Kimball / 1894.

Collation : Crown octavo, 7½ × 5; pp. viii + 156 + 16 pp. adv.; consisting of Frontispiece; Title-page; *Prefatory Note* by Alice Meynell, pp. iii—v; Contents, Text, and Advertisements.

Issued in red buckram lettered in gold.

Published price, 5s.

The English Edition consisted of 500 copies.

(107)

[PATMORE : Poetry of Pathos and Delight : 1896]

The Poetry of / Pathos & Delight / From the Works of / Coventry Patmore / [*Ornament*] / Passages Selected by / Alice Meynell / With a Portrait after J. S. Sargent, A.R.A. / London : William Heineman / MDCCCXCVI

Collation : Post octavo, 6⅞ × 4¼; pp. xvi + 136; consisting of Half-title; Frontispiece; Title-page; *Introductory Note* by Alice Meynell, pp. v—xi; etc.

Issued in decorative green cloth.

(108)

[BROWNING : Prometheus Bound : 1896]

Prometheus Bound/And Other Poems By/Elizabeth Barrett Browning / With an Introduction

/ By Alice Meynell / London: Ward, Lock & Bowden, Ltd. / New York and Melbourne. MDCCCXCVI

Collation: Crown octavo, 7½ × 4½; pp. xx + 332; consisting of Half-title; Frontispiece; Title-page, in red and black, as above; Introduction by Alice Meynell, pp. v—xv; etc.

Issued in red (later, green) cloth, gilt; top edge gilt.

Published price, 2s 6d.

(109)

[THE FLOWER OF THE MIND: 1897]

The Flower / Of the Mind / A Choice Among the best Poems / Made By / Alice Meynell / [*Ornament*] / London / Grant Richards / 9 Henrietta Street / 1897

Collation: Crown octavo, 7½ × 5; pp. xxiv + 348; consisting of Half-title; Title; Introduction by Alice Meynell (pp. v—viii); Contents, pp. xv—xxiv; Text and Notes, pp. 1—348.

Issued in light green buckram, gilt. Top edges gilt.

Published price, 6s.

(110)

[ST. AUGUSTINE: Confessions: 1900]

The Confessions / of / Saint Augustine / Edited by / Temple Scott / With an Introduction by /

Alice Meynell / [*Ornament*] / London / Grant Richards / 1900

Collation: Post octavo, 6⅝ × 4½; pp. 4 + xiv + 284; consisting of Blank leaf; Half-title; Title-page, in red and black; *Introduction*; *Preface* by Alice Meynell, pp. [v]—x.

Issued in stiff white parchment boards.

Published price, 1s.

(111)

[JOHN RUSKIN: 1900]

John Ruskin / By / Mrs Meynell / William Blackwood and Sons / Edinburgh and London / MDCCCC / *All Rights reserved*

Collation: Crown octavo, 7⅜ × 4¾; pp. viii + 300; consisting of Half-title; Title; Dedication; *Contents*; *Introduction* by Alice Meynell, pp. [1]—9; etc.

Issued in blue buckram, lettered and ornamented in white.

(112)

[PETRARCH: LOVE'S CRUCIFIX: 1902]

Love's Crucifix · Nine / Sonnets and a can- / zone · from Petrarch / By Alice Tobin · With / A Preface by Alice / Meynell · Illustrated / By Graham Robertson / [*Ornament*] / London: William Heineman: 1902

Collation : Quarto, $9\frac{3}{4} \times 7\frac{5}{8}$; pp. 32; consisting of Half-title; Title-page, in green and black; Preface by Alice Meynell, pp. [v—viii]; there are ten full page illustrations.

Issued in ornamental parchment wrappers.

(113)

[WORDSWORTH : Poems : 1903]

Poems by / William Wordsworth / With an Introduction by / Alice Meynell / Blackie and Son Limited London MCMIII

Collation : Foolscap octavo, $6 \times 3\frac{7}{8}$; pp. xii + 278; consisting of Half-title; Frontispiece; Decorative Title-page; Introduction by Alice Meynell, pp. v—viii; etc.

Issued in green cloth and in red leather, gilt; decorative end papers; top edge gilt.

Published price : cloth, 1s 6d; leather, 2s 6d.

(114)

[TENNYSON : Poems : 1903]

Poems by / Alfred Lord Tennyson / With an Introduction by / Alice Meynell / Blackie and Son Limited London MCMIII

Collation : Foolscap octavo, $6 \times 3\frac{7}{8}$; pp. xii + 278; consisting of Half-title; Frontispiece; Decorative title-page; Introduction by Alice Meynell, pp. v—vii, etc.

Issued in green cloth and in red leather, gilt; decorative end papers; top edge gilt.

Published price: cloth, 1s 6d; leather, 2s 6d.

(115)

[ELIZABETH BROWNING: Poems: 1903]

Poems By / Elizabeth Barrett Browning / With an Introduction by / Alice Meynell / Blackie and Son Limited London MCMIII

Collation: Foolscap octavo, 6 × 3⅞; pp. xii + 278; consisting of Half-title; Frontispiece; Decorative Title-page; Introduction by Alice Meynell, pp. v—vii; etc.

Issued in green cloth and in red leather gilt; top edges gilt; decorative end papers.

Published price: cloth, 1s 6d; leather, 2s 6d.

(116)

[ROBERT BROWNING: Poems: 1903]

Poems by / Robert Browning / With an Intro-duction by / Alice Meynell / Blackie and Son Limited London MCMIII

Collation: Foolscap octavo, 6 × 3⅞; pp. xii + 278; consisting of Half-title; Frontispiece; Decorative title-page; Introduction by Alice Meynell, pp. v—viii; etc.

Issued in green cloth and in red leather, gilt; decorative end papers; top edge gilt.

Published price: cloth, 1s 6d; leather, 2s 6d.

(117)

[SHELLEY: Poems: 1903]

Poems by / Percy Bysshe Shelley / With an Introduction by / Alice Meynell / Blackie and Son Limited London MCMIII

Collation: Foolscap octavo, 6 × 3⅞; pp. xii + 278; consisting of Half-title; Frontispiece; Decorative title-page; Introduction by Alice Meynell, pp. v—viii, etc.

Issued in green cloth and in red leather, gilt; decorative end papers; top edge gilt.

Published price: cloth, 1s 6d; leather, 2s 6d.

(118)

[KEATS: Poems: 1903]

Poems by / John Keats / With an Introduction by / Alice Meynell / Blackie and Son Limited London MCMIII

Collation: Foolscap octavo, 6 × 3⅞; pp. xii + 278; consisting of Half-title; Frontispiece; Decorative title-page; Introduction by Alice Meynell, pp. v—viii; etc.

Issued in green cloth and in red leather, gilt; decorative end papers; top edge gilt.

Published price : cloth, 1s 6d; leather, 2s 6d.

(119)

[SARGENT : Works : 1903]

The Work of / John S. Sargent / R.A. / With an Introductory Note / By / Mrs Meynell / [*Publishers' device*] / London / William Heinemann / New York : Charles Scribner's Sons / MCMIII

Collation : Folio, 17½ × 13; pp. 24 + illustrations; consisting of Half-title; Frontispiece; Title-page, in black and brown; *Introductory Note* by Mrs Meynell, pp. [5—18]; etc.

Published price, £6 6s.

(120)

[A SEVENTEENTH CENTURY ANTHOLOGY : 1904]

A / Seventeenth / Century / Anthology / [*Ornament*] / With an Introduction by / Alice Meynell / Blackie & Son Ld London.

Collation : Foolscap octavo, 6 × 3⅞; pp. xvi + 332; consisting of Half-title; Frontispiece; Decorative title-page; Introduction by Alice Meynell, pp. iii—vii, etc.

Issued in green cloth, and red leather gilt; decorative end papers; top edges gilt.

Published price : cloth, 1s 6d; leather, 2s 6d.

(121)

[CHAPMAN : A Little Child's Wreath : 1904]

A Little Child's Wreath / By Elizabeth Rachel / Chapman. With Illus - / trations by W. Graham / Robertson and a Pre- / face by Alice Meynell / John Lane : Publisher/ London and New York / MDCCCCIV

Collation : Duodecimo, 5½ × 4⅜; pp. 72, consisting of Half-title; Frontispiece; Title-page; Dedication; *Introductory Note* by Alice Meynell, pp. 9—15, etc.

Issued in olive green cloth and in leather, also in blue wrappers.

Published price, 1s; 1s 6d in leather.

(122)

[TENNYSON : In Memoriam : 1904]

In Memoriam / By / Alfred Lord Tennyson / With an Analysis by / The Rev. F. W. Robertson / And an Introduction by / Alice Meynell / Blackie & Son Ld London

Collation : Foolscap octavo, 6 × 3⅞; pp. 4 + x + 232; consisting of Half-title; Frontispiece; Decorative title-page; Introduction by Alice Meynell, pp. iii—x; etc.

Issued in green cloth and in red leather, gilt; decorative end papers; top edge gilt.

Published price: cloth, 1s 6d; leather, 2s 6d.

(123)

[THE CHILDHOOD OF CHRIST: 1904]

The Gospel of the / Childhood of Our / Lord
Jesus Christ / Translated From the Latin / By
Henry Copley Greene / With Original Text of
the Manu- / script At the Monastery of Saint /
Wolfgang, An Introduction by Alice Meynell,
And a Cover and / Illustrations by Carlos
Schwabe / New York : Scott-Thaw Co. / Lon-
don : Burns and Oates / MCMIV

Collation : Foolscap octavo, 6⅜ × 4⅞; pp. 272; consisting
of blank leaf; Half-title; Title-page; Fly-title;
Illustrations; p. [11], Poem; Introduction by Alice
Meynell, pp. 13—21; etc.

Issued in blue-grey pictorial boards. Also in dark blue
leather.

There was an edition of 25 copies on Japanese vellum
printed for subscribers. The above edition is on Chelten-
ham woven paper and is limited to 1000 copies. Printed
in Boston, U.S.A.

(124)

[HERRICK: Poems: 1905]

Poems / By / Robert Herrick / [*ornament*] /
With an Introduction by / Alice Meynell /
Blackie & Son Ltd London

Collation : Foolscap octavo, 6 × 3⅞; pp. xvi + 374;
consisting of Half-title; Frontispiece; Decorative
Title-page; Introduction by Alice Meynell, pp. iii—
vi; etc.

I

Issued in green cloth and in red leather, gilt; floreated
end papers; top edges gilt.

Published price: cloth, 1s 6d; leather, 2s 6d.

(125)

[COLERIDGE: Poems: 1905]

Poems / By / Samuel Taylor / Coleridge / With
an Introduction by / Alice Meynell / Blackie &
Son Ld London

Collation: Foolscap octavo, 6 × 3⅞; pp. xii + 316
(including blank leaf); consisting of Half-title;
Frontispiece; Decorative Title-page; Introduction
by Alice Meynell, pp. iii—viii, etc.

Issued in green cloth, and in red leather, gilt; decorative
end papers; top edges gilt.

Published price: cloth, 1s 6d; leather, 2s 6d.

(126)

[COWPER: Poems: 1905]

Poems / By / William Cowper / [*Ornament*] /
With an Introduction by / Alice Meynell /
Blackie & Son Ld London

Collation: Foolscap octavo, 6 × 3⅞; pp. x + 392;
consisting of Half-title; Frontispiece; Decorative
Title-page; Introduction by Alice Meynell, pp. iii—
viii, etc.

Issued in green cloth, and in red leather, gilt; decorative end papers; top edges gilt.

Published price: cloth, 1s 6d; leather, 2s 6d.

(127)

[PATMORE : Angel in the House, etc: 1905]

The Angel in the House / Together with / The Victories of Love / By / Coventry Patmore / With an Introduction by / Alice Meynell / [*Ornament*] / London / George Routledge & Sons, Limited / New York: E. P. Dutton & Co.

Collation: Foolscap octavo, 5⅛ × 3¾; pp. xvi + 336; consisting of Half-title; Title-page; Note; Dedication; Contents, pp. ix—xvi; Introduction by Alice Meynell, pp. [1]—26; etc.

Issued in cloth and in leather.

Published price, 1s; and in leather, price 2s.

(128)

[ARNOLD : Poems : 1906]

Poems / By / Matthew Arnold / With an Introduction by / Alice Meynell / Blackie & Son Ltd London

Collation: Foolscap octavo, 6 × 3⅞; pp. xii + 360; consisting of Half-title; Frontispiece; Decorative Title-page; Introduction by Alice Meynell, pp. iii—vii; etc.

Issued in green cloth and in red leather, gilt; decorative end papers; top edges gilt.

Published price: cloth, 1s 6d; leather, 2s 6d.

(129)

[ROSSETTI : Poems : 1906]

Poems / By / Christina / Rossetti / With an Introduction by / Alice Meynell / Blackie and Son Ld London

Collation : Foolscap octavo, 6 × 3⅞; pp. 200; consisting of Half-title; Frontispiece; Decorative Title-page; Introduction by Alive Meynell, pp. 3—7, etc.

Issued in green cloth and in red leather, gilt; decorative end papers; top edges gilt.

Published price: cloth, 1s 6d; leather, 2s 6d.

(130)

[TABB : Poems : 1906]

A Selection from / The Verses of / John B. Tabb / Made by Alice Meynell / Burns and Oates / 28 Orchard Street / London W

Collation : Foolscap octavo; pp. x + 120. (Page ix misprinted xi.)

Issued in orange cloth.

Published price, 2s 6d.

(131)

[STOKES : Exhibition : 1907)

An Exhibition of Pictures / Painted in Austria-Hungary / By Adrian & Marianne Stokes / With a Prefatory Note by / Alice Meynell / Ernest Brown & Phillips / The Leicester Galleries / Leicester Square, London / March - April, 1907.

Collation: Foolscap octavo, 5¾ × 4⅜; pp. 16; Introduction by Mrs Meynell, pp. 3—7, etc.

Issued in light green wrappers.

(132)

[SHAKESPEARE : Taming of the Shrew : 1907]

The Complete Works / of / William Shakespeare / With Annotations and a General / Introduction / By Sidney Lee / Vol.VII / The Taming of the Shrew / With a Special Introduction by / Alice Meynell / and an Original Frontispiece by / Eleanor F. Brickdale / New York / George D. Sproul / 1907

Collation : Imperial octavo, 11⅛ × 8¼; pp. 4 + xx + 128; consisting of 4 pp. blank; Fly-title; Half-title; Frontispiece; Title-page, as above, in red and black; Contents; Introduction by Alice Meynell, pp. ix—xx; etc.

Issued in light green boards backed with dark green cloth; white paper label on back.

Printed in America where it was first issued. The English edition bears a slip of endorsement pasted to the title-page over the last three lines: *London / George G. Harrap & Company / 15 York Street Covent Garden W.C.*

(133)

[INGELOW : Poems : 1908]

Poems / By / Jean Ingelow / With an Introduction by / Alice Meynell / Blackie & Son Ltd London

Collation: Foolscap octavo, 6 × 3⅞; pp. viii + 314; consisting of Half-title; Frontispiece; Decorative Title-page; Introduction by Alice Meynell, pp. iii— vi, etc.

Issued in green cloth and in red leather, gilt, floreated end papers; top edges gilt.

Published price: cloth, 1s 6d; leather, 2s 6d.

(134)

[YONGE : Heir of Redclyffe : 1909]

The Heir of / Redclyffe / By Charlotte / M. Yonge / [*Everyman device*] / London: Published / by J. M. Dent & Co / and in New York / By E. P. Dutton & Co

Collation: Post octavo, 6⅞ × 4¼; pp. xii + 576; consisting of Half-title; Decorative page; Decorative title-page; Introduction by Alice Meynell, pp. vii—xi; etc.

Issued in red cloth and in red leather; gilt on spine; top edge green.

Published price: cloth, 1s; leather, 2s.

(135)

[CASHMORE: The Mount of Vision: 1910]

The Mount of / Vision / A Book of English / Mystic Verse / Selected and Arranged / By / Adeline Cashmore / With an Introduction / By / Alice Meynell / London / Chapman and Hall, Limited.

Collation: Post octavo, $7\frac{5}{16}$ × $4\frac{1}{2}$; pp. xxii + 160; consisting of Half-title; Title-page; Dedication leaf; *Acknowledgments*; *The Mystical Lyric*, by Alice Meynell, pp. ix—xvii.

Issued in pale-green buckram gilt; top edges gilt.

Published price, 2s 6d.

(136)

[RUSKIN: Seven Lamps of Architecture: 1910]

Mrs. Alice Meynell / Introduces the Treatise on the / *Seven Lamps of Archi-* / *Tecture,* with the Author's / illustrations, by John RUSKIN, born / in 1819, died in 1900, as the ninth / volume in the series of Books that / marked Epochs, published in the year / 1910 by George Rout - / Ledge & Sons, Limited.

Collation: Foolscap octavo, $6\frac{3}{8} \times 4$; pp. xxxvi + 236; consisting of Half-title; Frontispiece; Title-page; *Contents*; List of Plates; etc. Introduction by Alice Meynell occupies pp. xxi—xxxv.

Issued in blue buckram backed with corners of white parchment; gilt; top edges gilt.

Published price, 2s 6d.

(137)

[JOHNSON: Selections: 1911]

The Regent Library / Samuel Johnson / By Alice Meynell and / G. K. Chesterton / London / Herbert & Daniel / 21 Maddox Street / W.

Collation: Foolscap octavo, $6\frac{1}{4} \times 4\frac{5}{8}$; pp. xx + 266; consisting of Half-title; Frontispiece; Decorative Title-page; etc. The Introduction, pp. vii—xx, is by Chesterton.

Issued in buff cloth, gilt, and in leather; decorative end papers.

Published price: cloth, 2s 6d; leather, 3s 6d.

(138)

[BLAKE: Poems: 1911]

Poems / By / William / Blake / Selected with / an Introduction by / Alice Meynell / Blackie and Son Ld London

Collation: Foolscap octavo, 6 × 4; pp. xvi + 226; consisting of Half-title; Frontispiece; Decorative Title-page; Introduction by Alice Meynell, pp. iii—xii; etc.

Issued in green cloth and in red leather, gilt; decorative end papers; top edge gilt.

Published price: cloth, 1s 6d; leather, 2s.

(139)

[THE MYSTICS, 17TH CENTURY]

The Mystics / Seventeenth Century / Chosen by / Alice Meynell / [*Ornament*] / London / Alexander Moring, Ltd / 32 George Street / Hanover Square, W

Collation: Small octavo, 4⅝ × 2⅞; pp. iv + 92.

Issued in red cloth and in leather, gilt.

Published price: cloth, 6d; leather, 1s.

(140)

[BROWNING: Art of Scansion: 1916]

The Art / of / Scansion / By / Elizabeth Barrett Browning / With an Introduction / By / Alice Meynell / London / [Privately printed by Clement Shorter, December 1916]

Collation: Quarto, 9 × 8½; pp. 2 + x + 16; consisting of Blank leaf; Half-title, *The Art of / Scansion,* verso blank; Title-page, as above, within ruled border verso blank; *Preface,* verso blank; *Intro-duction,* by Alice Meynell, pp. vii—ix, verso blank; Text, pp. 1—[12] ; Notice, p. [13], verso blank; pp. [15—16], blank.

Issued in bright green wrappers; on the front is repro-duced the title-page.

The Edition consists of 25 copies.

(141)

[WATSON : Selected Essays : 1919]

Selected Essays / and Reviews / Also His Last Letter from the Front / By / Herbert Coleridge Watson / With an Introduction by / Alice Mey-nell / *With two Portraits and Illustrations from Photographs / taken by the Author.* / [*Orna-ment*] / Bedford : F. R. Hockliffe / 1919

Collation : Crown octavo, $7\frac{5}{8} \times 5\frac{1}{8}$; pp. 6 + 114 (including blank at end) ; consisting of Half-title ; Frontispiece ; Title-page ; Contents ; Introduction by Alice Meynell, p. 1—3, etc.

Issued in blue boards, linen backed, with paper label on back.

Published price, 6s.

(142)

[THE SCHOOL OF POETRY : 1923]

The / School of Poetry / An Anthology / *Chosen for Young Readers by* / Alice Meynell / [*Pub-*

lisher's device] / London : 48 Pall Mall / W. Collins Sons & Co, Ltd. / Glasgow Melbourne Auckland

Collation : Large octavo, $8\frac{1}{8} \times 5\frac{5}{8}$; pp. 242 + 6 ; consisting of Half-title; Portrait of Alice Meynell; Title-page, in blue and black; Introduction by Alice Meynell, etc.

Issued in blue cloth; also edition-de-luxe in leather.

WALTER HORATIO PATER

1839—1894

WALTER PATER

PART I: COMPLETE BOOKS

(143)

[Studies in the History of the Renaissance : 1873.]

Studies / In the History of the / Renaissance / By / Walter H. Pater / Fellow of Brasenose College, Oxford / London / Macmillan and Co. / 1873 / [*All rights reserved*]

Collation: Demy octavo, 7⅛ × 5⅛; pp. xvi + 216; consisting of Half-title, *Studies / In the History of the / Renaissance,* verso, publishers' device; Title-page, as above, verso blank; *To C.L.S.* [hadwell], verso blank; *Preface,* pp. [vii]—xiv; *Contents.,* verso blank; Text, pp. [1]—213, verso, *Oxford: By T. Combe, M.A., E. B. Gardner, E. Pickard Hall, and J. H. Stacey, Printers to the University.*; Advertisements, pp. [215—6]. Headlines throughout : verso, *The Renaissance*; recto, various.

Signatures : [A]—O, by 8s; P, 4 leaves.

Issued in green cloth lettered in gold on back, *Studies / In the History / of the / Renaissance / — / W. H. Pater*; chocolate end papers. The book is printed on ribbed paper.

Published price, 7s 6d.

129

Contents : *Aucassin and Nicolette* (entitled *Two Early French Stories* in later editions); *Pico della Mirandola* (reprinted from *Fortnightly Review* for October, 1871); *Sandro Botticelli* (from *Fortnightly Review* for August, 1870); *Luca della Robbia*; *Poetry of Michelangelo* (reprinted from *Fortnightly Review* for November, 1871); *Leonardo da Vinci* (from *Fortnightly Review* for November, 1869); *Joachim du Bellay*; *Winkelmann* (from *Westminster Review* for January, 1867); and *Conclusion.*

The third edition (1888) includes *The School of Giorgione* (from *Fortnightly Review* for October, 1877). (Published price, 10s 6d.)

(144)

[Marius the Epicurean : 1885]

Marius the Epicurean / His Sensations and Ideas / By / Walter Pater, M.A. / Fellow of Brasenose College, Oxford / χειμερινὸς ὄνειρος ὅτε μήκισται αἱ νύκτες / Volume I [*II*] / London : / Macmillan and Co. / 1885 / [*All rights reserved*]

Collation : 2 vols., Demy octavo, 8 × 5⅝.

Volume I : pp. viii + 260; consisting of Half-title, *Marius the Epicurean*, verso, *By the same Author*; Title-page, as above, verso blank; Dedication, verso blank; Contents, verso blank; Text, including Fly-titles, pp. [1]—260. Headlines throughout, *Marius the Epicurean.*

Signatures : a, 4 leaves; B—R, by 8s; S, 2 leaves.

Volume II : pp. viii + 248; consisting of p. [i], blank, verso, *By the same Author*; Half-title, *Marius the Epicurean*, verso blank; Title-page, as above, verso blank; Contents, verso blank; Text, including Fly-titles, pp. [1]—246; imprint, p. [247], *Oxford Printed by Horace Hart, Printer to the University*, verso blank. Headlines throughout, *Marius the Epicurean*.

Signatures : a, 4 leaves; B—P, by 8s; R, 4 leaves.

Issued in blue cloth lettered in gold on back, *Marius / The / Epicurean / Vol I* [II] */ Walter / Pater / Macmillan / and Co.*

Published price, 21s.

(145)

[IMAGINARY PORTRAITS : 1887]

Imaginary Portraits / By / Walter Pater, M.A. / Fellow of Brasenose College, Oxford / London / Macmillan and Co. / and New York / 1887 / *All rights reserved*

Collation : Demy octavo, 8⅛ × 5⅜; pp. viii + 184; consisting of Half-title, *Imaginary Portraits*, verso, *By the same Author*; Title-page, as above, verso, *Printed by R. & R. Clark, Edinburgh*; *Contents*, verso blank; Fly-title, *I. / A Prince of Court Painters*, verso blank; Text, including other fly-titles, pp. [1]—180; imprint at foot; Advertisements, pp. [181—4]. Headlines throughout : verso, *Imaginary Portraits*; recto varying.

Signatures : [A], 4 leaves; B—M, by 8s; N, 4 leaves.

K

Issued in blue cloth lettered in gold on back, *Imaginary / Portraits / Walter / Pater / Macmillan / and Co.*

Published price, 6s.

Contents : *A Prince of Court Painters* (reprinted from *Macmillan's Magazine* for October, 1885); *Denys l'Auxerrois* (from *Macmillan's Magazine* for October, 1886); *Sebastian van Storck* (from *Macmillan's Magazine* for March, 1886); and *Duke Carl of Rosenmold* (from *Macmillan's Magazine* for May, 1887).

(146)

[APPRECIATIONS : 1889]

Appreciations / With an Essay on Style / By / Walter Pater / Fellow of Brasenose College / London / Macmillan and Co. / and New York / 1889 / *All rights reserved*

Collation : Demy octavo, $8\frac{1}{8}$ × $5\frac{3}{8}$; pp. viii + 264; consisting of Half-title, *Appreciations*, verso *By the same Author.*; Title-page, as above, verso blank; Dedication, verso blank; *Contents*, verso blank; Text, pp. [1]—264, imprint at foot, *Printed by R. & R. Clark, Edinburgh.* Headlines throughout : verso, *Appreciation*; recto, various.

Signatures : [A], 4 leaves; B—R, by 8s; S, 4 leaves.

Issued in blue cloth lettered in gold on back, *Appreciations / With an Essay / On Style / Walter / Pater / Macmillan / and Co.*

Published price, 8s 6d.

Contents: *Style* (reprinted from *Fortnightly Review* for December, 1888); *Wordsworth* (from *Fortnightly Review* for April, 1874); *Coleridge* (from *Westminster Review* for January, 1866); *Charles Lamb* (from *Fortnightly Review* for October, 1878); *Sir Thomas Browne* (written in 1886); *Love's Labour Lost* (from *Macmillan's Magazine* for December, 1878); *Measure for Measure* (from *Fortnightly Review* for November, 1874); *Shakspere's English Kings*; *Aesthetic Poetry* (written in 1868); *Dante Gabriel Rossetti* (written in 1883); *Postscript* (published in *Macmillan's* for November, 1876, under the title of *Romanticism*).

The *Second Edition, 1890,* omits *Aesthetic Poetry* (which is not included in the *Collected Works*) and includes a paper on *Feuillet's "La Morte"* (written in 1886).

(147)

[PLATO AND PLATONISM: 1893]

Plato and Platonism / A Series of Lectures / By / Walter Pater / Fellow of Brasenose College / Ὡς φιλοσοφίας μέν οὔσης μεγίστης μουσικῆς / London / Macmillan and Co. / and New York / 1893 / [*All rights reserved*]

Collation: Demy octavo, 8⅛ × 5⅜; pp. viii + 260; consisting of Half-title, *Plato and Platonism*, verso, *By the same Author.*; Title-page as above, verso, publishers' device in centre, at foot, *Oxford: Horace Hart, Printer to the University*; Foreword by the author, p. [v], verso blank; *Contents*, verso blank; Text, pp. [1]—259, verso, printers' imprint repeated.

Headlines throughout; verso, *Plato and Platonism*, recto varying. There are 10 lectures.

Signatures : [A], 4 leaves; B—R by 8s; S, 2 leaves.

Issued in blue cloth lettered in gold on the back only, *Plato / and / Platonism / Walter / Pater / Macmillan / and Co.*

Published price, 8s 6d.

Chapters I, VI and VIII are reprinted from periodicals, where they had appeared under different titles, respectively, as follows : *A Chapter of Plato* (*Macmillan's Magazine* for May, 1892); *The Genius of Plato* (*Contemporary Review* for February, 1892); *Lacedaemon* (*Contemporary Review* for June, 1892).

(148)

[AN IMAGINARY PORTRAIT : 1894]

An Imaginary Portrait / By Walter Pater [*Ornaments*]

Collation: Small octavo, $6\frac{5}{8} \times 4\frac{5}{8}$; pp. xii + 64 + 8; consisting of 4 blank leaves; Half-title; *An / Imaginary Portrait / By Walter Pater*, verso blank; p. [xi] blank, verso, *250 Copies printed. This is No.* ; Title-page, as above, verso blank; Fly-title, *The Child in / The House*, verso blank; Text, pp. 5—61, verso, ornament; p. [63], blank, verso Ornamental design and *Printed by H. Daniel: Oxford: 1894*; 4 blank leaves. Headlines throughout: verso, *The Child*; recto, *In the House*.

Signatures unsigned but make up as follows : [A], 4 leaves; [B], 2; [C]—[F], by 8s; [G], 4 leaves.

Issued in blue grey wrappers (6⅛ × 4⅞) lettered in black on front cover, *An / Imaginary Portrait / By Walter Pater.*

Reprinted from *Macmillan's Magazine* for August, 1878. Later included in *Miscellaneous Studies,* 1895.

(149)

[GREEK STUDIES : 1895]

Greek Studies / A Series of Essays / By / Walter Pater / Late Fellow of Brasenose College / Prepared for the Press / By / Charles L. Shadwell / Fellow of Oriel College / London / Macmillan & Co. / and New York / 1895 / [*All rights reserved*]

Collation: Demy octavo, 8⅛ × 5⅜; pp. xii + 316; consisting of Half-title, *Greek Studies,* verso publisher's device; Frontispiece and guard; Title-page, as above, verso *Oxford Horace Hart, Printer to the University*; *Preface*, dated *Oct. 1894.*, pp. [v]—ix, verso blank; *Contents*, verso blank; Text, pp. [1]—315, verso, imprint. Headlines throughout varying with text.

Signatures: [A], 6 leaves, B—V, by 8s; X, 6 leaves.

Issued in blue cloth lettered in gold on the back, *Greek / Studies / Walter / Pater / Macmillan / and Co.*

Published price, 10s 6d.

Contents: *A Study of Dionysus* (reprinted from *Fortnightly Review* for December, 1876); *The Bacchanals of Euripides* (from *Macmillan's Magazine* for May, 1878); *The Myth of Demeter and Persephone* (from *Fortnightly Review* for January and February, 1875); *Hippolytus Veiled* (from *Macmillan's Magazine* for ·August, 1889); *The Beginnings of Greek Sculpture* (from *Fortnightly Review* for February and March, 1880); *The Marbles of Aegina* (from *Fortnightly Review* for April, 1880); and *The Age of Athletic Prizemen* (from *Contemporary Review* for February, 1894).

C. L. Shadwell states (*Miscellaneous Studies,* 1895) that Pater's essay on the Bacchanals of Euripides was published in Tyrell's edition (1892). This is an error which Wright repeats in his Life of Pater. The first and various successive Macmillan editions of Tyrell reveal no touch of Pater's hand.

(150)

[MISCELLANEOUS STUDIES : 1895]

Miscellaneous / Studies / A Series of Essays / By / Walter Pater / Late Fellow of Brasenose College / Prepared For the Press / By / Charles L. Shadwell / Fellow of Oriel College / London / Macmillan and Co. / and New York / 1895 / [*All rights reserved*]

Collation: Demy octavo, 8 × 5½; pp. xvi + 260; consisting of Half-title, *Miscellaneous Studies,* verso, publisher's device; Title-page as above, verso *Oxford Horace Hart, Printer to the University; Preface,* pp. [v]—xiv, dated *August, 1895.; Contents,* verso blank; Text, pp. [1]—259, verso, printers' imprint repeated. Headlines throughout; varying with text. There are ten essays.

Signatures: [A]—R, by 8s; S, 2 leaves.

Issued in dark blue cloth lettered in gold on the back only, *Miscellaneous / Studies / Walter / Pater / Macmillan / and Co.* There was a pale green dust wrapper.

Published price, 9s.

Contents: *Prosper Mérimée* (reprinted from *Fortnightly Review* for December, 1890); *Raphael* (from *Fortnightly Review* for October, 1892); *Pascal* (from *Contemporary Review* for December, 1894); *Art Notes in North Italy* (from *New Review* for November, 1890); *Notre-Dame d'Amiens* (from *Nineteenth Century* for March, 1894); *Vézelay* (from *Nineteenth Century* for June, 1894); *Apollo in Picardy* (from *Harper's Magazine* for November, 1893); *The Child in the House* (from *Macmillan's Magazine* for August, 1878); *Emerald Uthwart* (from *New Review* for June and July, 1892); and *Diaphaneitè* (written in 1867).

(151)

[Gaston De Latour: 1896]

Gaston De Latour / An Unfinished Romance / By / Walter Pater / Late Fellow of Brasenose College / Prepared for the Press by / Charles L. Shadwell / Fellow of Oriel College / London / MacMillan and Co., Ltd. / New York: The MacMillan Co. / 1896 / [*All rights reserved*]

Collation: Demy octavo, 8 × 5⅜; pp. 2 + x + 200; consisting of blank leaf; Half-title, *Gaston De*

Latour, verso, publisher's device; Title-page, as above, verso *Oxford Horace Hart, Printer to the University*; Preface, dated *July, 1896.*, pp. [v]—vii, verso blank; *Contents*, verso blank; Text, pp. [1]—200, imprint at foot. Headlines throughout : verso, *Gaston De Latour.*; recto, various.

Signatures : a, 6 leaves; B—N, by 8s; O, 4 leaves.

Issued in blue cloth lettered in gold on back, *Gaston / De / Latour / Walter / Pater / Macmillan / and Co.*

Published price, 7s 6d.

Reprinted from *Macmillan's Magazine* for 1888 : Chapter I, from the June Issue; II, July; III, August; IV, September; V, October. An article which appeared in *Fortnightly Review* for August, 1889, (entitled *Giordano Bruno*) was originally intended to form chapter VII, and is included here; Chapter VI is mostly from MSS. sources.

(152)

[Essays from the " Guardian " : 1896]

Essays / From / The " Guardian " / By / Walter Pater / Late Fellow of Brazenose College / London / Printed for Private Circulation / at the Chiswick Press / 1896

Collation : Foolscap octavo, $7\frac{1}{8} \times 4\frac{3}{8}$; pp. viii + 164; consisting of Half-title, [Ornament] / *Essays from the / " Guardian "* / [Ornament], verso Notice of Limitation; Title-page, in red and black, as above, verso blank; *Preface* [By Edmund Gosse] pp. [v]—vi; *Contents*, verso blank; Text, including Fly-titles,

ESSAYS

FROM

THE "GUARDIAN"

BY

WALTER PATER

LATE FELLOW OF BRAZENOSE COLLEGE

LONDON

PRINTED FOR PRIVATE CIRCULATION

AT THE CHISWICK PRESS

1896

Facsimile, actual size of type, of Title-page of No. 152.

f.p. 138

pp. [1]—163, verso, ornament and imprint. Headlines throughout; verso, *Essays from*; recto, *the
" Guardian ".*

Signatures : [A], 4 leaves; B—L, by 8s; M, 2 leaves.

Issued in light blue boards with paper label on back,
reading *Essays / from the / Guardian / — / By /
Walter / Pater.*

The essays have all been published in the " Guardian ",
as follows : *English Literature,* in the issue for Feb.
17, 1886; *Amiel's "Journal Intime",* March 17, 1886;
Browning, Nov. 9, 1887; *'Robert Elsmere',* March 28,
1888; *Their Majesties' Servants,* June 27, 1888; *Wordsworth,* Feb. 27, 1889; *Mr. Gosse's Poems,* Oct. 29, 1890;
Ferdinand Fabre, June 12, 1889; *The "Contes" of M.
Augustin Filon,* July 16, 1890.

(153)

[WORKS : 1900—1]

This First Collected Edition (VIII vols.;
Essays from the " Guardian " published uniform
with the set may be considered Vol. IX), contains
no new material.

* * *

There have been separate reprints *Mérimée; Coleridge,*
etc., which are not listed, being merely reprints and of
no value to the collector or scholar. *Emerald Uthwart*
was privately printed for the *King's School,* Canterbury,
in 1905.

PART II:

BOOKS WITH AN INTRODUCTION

BY WALTER PATER

(154)

[DANTE: The Purgatory: 1892]

The / Purgatory / of / Dante Alighieri / (Purgatorio I—XXVII) / An Experiment in / Literal Verse Translation / By / Charles Lancelot Shadwell, M.A., B.C.L. / Fellow of Oriel College, Oxford / With an Introduction / By / Walter Pater, M.A. / Fellow of Brasenose College, Oxford. / London / MacMillan and Co. / and New York / 1892

Collation: Crown octavo, 8⅛ × 5⅜; pp. xxviii + 412; consisting of Half-title; Title (in yellow and black); *Preface*, pp. [v]—xii; *Introduction* by Walter Pater, pp. [xiii]—xxviii, etc.

Issued in white parchment, gilt.

Published price, 10s.

FRANCIS JOSEPH THOMPSON

1859—1907

FRANCIS THOMPSON

(155)

[JOHN BAPTIST DE LA SALLE : 1891]

The Life and Labours / Of / Blessed John Baptist de la Salle, / Founder of the Brothers of the Christian Schools, / and Father of Modern Popular Education. / [*Double rule*] / By Francis Thompson / [*Double rule*] / With Thirteen Illustrations. / [*Double rule*] / London. / John Sinkins, 43, Essex Street, Strand, W.C

Collation : Demy octavo; pp. vii + 80; consisting of Title-page, as above, verso blank; pp. [ii—iii]; *Preface.*, pp. [iv—v] ; Frontispiece, [vi—vii]; Text, pp. [1]—78; pp. 79—80, Notices. Headlines throughout.

Signatures : [1], 3 leaves; 2—6, by eights.

Issued in pale green wrappers lettered in red; on the front cover is reproduced the title-page with the addition of *Being the Issue of Merry England for April, 1891.* / [Double rule.] There are advertisements on the back and on insides of wrappers; the inside front wrapper is p. [i].

Re-issued in 1911 with a preface by Wilfrid Meynell, Thompson's literary executor.

(156)

[CHILD SET IN THE MIDST : 1892]

The / Child Set in the Midst / By Modern Poets / (" And He took a little child and set him in the midst of them.") / Edited by Wilfrid Meynell. / - / *With a facsimile of the MS. of " The Toys,"* by Coventry Patmore. / [*Ornament*] / [*Printers'* *device*] / London : / The Leadenhall Press, Ltd : 50, Leadenhall Street, E.C. / *Simpkin, Marshall, Hamilton, Kent & Co., Ltd:* / - / *New York: Charles Scribners' Sons, 743 & 745, Broadway*

Collation : Post octavo, $7\frac{1}{4} \times 5$; pp. 12 + 196; consisting of blank leaf; Facsimile, pp. [3—4] ; Title-page, as above, verso imprint and ornament; Dedication, verso blank; *Contents.*, pp. [9—11'], verso Ornament; *Preface.*, pp. [i]—xxiii, verso Ornament; Text, pp. [25]—195, verso *Acknowledgment.* Headlines throughout, according to the author.

Signatures : 2 leaves unsigned; [A]—M, by 8s; N, 6 leaves.

Issued in black cloth with small gilt ornament on front cover; paper label on back reads [Double rule] / *The* / *Child* / *Set in* / *The Midst:* / *By Modern* / *Poets.* / *Edited by* / *Wilfrid Meynell.* / [Double rule].

Published price : post octavo edition, 6s; also royal 16mo edition, 3s 6d.

Poems by Francis Thompson pp. 183—195. There are 4 poems by him, his first to appear in book form.

POEMS
BY FRANCIS
THOMPSON

LONDON
ELKIN MATHEWS & JOHN LANE
BOSTON
COPELAND & DAY   1893

Yours truly

Francis Thompson.

May. 13, 1895.

Facsimile, actual size of design, of Title-page (in red in original) of No. 157, with inscription in the Author's hand. (By courtesy of Mr. Clement K. Shorter).

(157)

[POEMS : 1893]

Poems / By Francis / Thompson / [*Ornament*] / London / Elkin Mathews & John Lane / Boston / Copeland & Day / 1893

Collation : *Small Paper Copy* : Square octavo, 7¼ × 6⅜ ; pp. x + 84 + 16 pp. adv.; consisting of Half-title, *Poems.*, verso, Notice of Limitation; Frontispiece, Title-page, as above, printed in orange, verso blank; *Dedication.*, pp. [vii]—viii; *Contents.*, p. [ix], verso blank; Text, including Fly-titles, pp. [1]—81, verso blank; imprint within ornament, *Printed by R. Folkard & Son, 22, Devonshire St., Queen Sq., London.*, Advertisements dated *October, 1893.*, 16 pp.

Signatures : 1 leaf unsigned; [A], 4 leaves; 2 leaves unsigned [Title-page and frontis.]; B—F, by 8s; G, 2 leaves; 8 leaves adv.

Issued in slate coloured boards lettered in gold on back *Poems / By / Fran- / cis / Thomp- / Son / London / & Boston / 1893*; ornaments in gold on back and on front cover. Published price, 5s.

The edition consists of 500 copies.

Collation : *Large Paper Copy* : 8 × 6⅞ ; pp. 4 + x + 86; consisting of 2 blank leaves, pp. [1—4] ; Half-title, *Poems*, verso blank; collation follows that of the small paper copies, omitting the advertisements and adding a blank leaf at the end. Notice of limitation is in manuscript on the first blank page; it is initialed by Everard Meynell and by John Lane. Printed on Jap. vellum and signed by the author on the title-page.

Signatures : [A]—F, by 8s; G, 2 leaves.

Issued in cream coloured parchment boards, ornamented in gold on back, and on front and back covers; lettered in gold on back *Poems / By / Fran- / cis / Thomp- / Son.*

The Large Paper Edition consisted of 12 copies printed on Japanese vellum.

(158)

[Songs Wing to Wing : 1895]

Songs / Wing-to-Wing : / An Offering to Two Sisters. / By / Francis Thompson. / [*Double line*] */ Printed for Private Circulation. / [Double line*] / London : / Printed By the Westminster Press, 333 Harrow Road, W. / - / 1895.

Collation : Square octavo, 7¾ × 6⅝; pp. vi + 66; consisting of Half-title, *Songs / Wing- to- Wing: / An offering to Two Sisters.*, verso blank; *Preface*, dated *1895.*, verso blank; Text, pp. [1]—65, verso blank.

Signatures : [1], 3 leaves; 2—4 by 8s, 5, 9 leaves.

Issued in wrappers. The front cover has been described, as there is no full Title-page.

(159)

[Sister Songs : 1895]

Sister-Songs / An Offering to / Two Sisters . . . / By Francis Thompson / [*Ornament*] / London·

John Lane at the / Bodley Head Vigo Street / Boston · Copeland and Day / 1895

Collation: Square octavo, 7⅞ × 6½; pp. viii + 68 + 16 pp. adv.; consisting of Half-title, *Sister Songs*, verso, Notice; p. [iii], blank, verso, Frontispiece; Title-page, as above; printed in orange-red, verso blank; *Preface*, verso blank; Text, pp. [1]—65, verso blank; Advertisements, pp. [67—8]; 16 pp. Advertisements dated *1895*.

Signatures: [1], four leaves; 2—5, by eights; 6, two leaves; 8 leaves adv.

Issued in olive green buckram lettered in gold on back, *Sister / Songs / By / Fran- / cis / Thomp- / son. / The / Bodley Head / & Boston*; ornaments in gold on back and on front cover.

Published price, 5s.

First published edition of " Songs Wing to Wing " which was privately printed in the same year.

(160)

[CHÉRANCÉ: ST. ANTHONY: 1895]

St. Anthony of Padua / By / Father Leopold de Chérancé, / O.S.F.C. / *Rendered into English* / By / Father Marianus, O.S.F.C. / *With an Introduction* / By / Father Anselm, O.S.F.C. / [*ornament*] / London : Burns & Oates, Limited. / New York, Cincinnati, Chicago : Benziger Brothers.

Collation: Crown octavo, 7⅝ × 5; pp. xxviii + 220.

L

Issued in brown boards lettered in gold : on back, *St. / Anthony / of / Padua / ══ / Burns / & Oates / Ltd.*; on front cover, *St. Anthony / of Padua.*

Published price, 2s 6d.

To St. Anthony of Padua, a poem by Francis Thompson, is here first published (p. xvi).

(161)

[NEW POEMS : 1897]

New Poems / By / Francis Thompson / [*Ornament*] / Westminster / Archibald Constable and Co. / 1897

Collation : Crown octavo, 7⅝ × 5⅛; pp. viii + 224; consisting of Half-title, *New Poems / By Francis Thompson*, verso blank; Title-page, as above, verso *Edinburgh: T. and A. Constable, Printers to Her Majesty*; *Contents*, pp. [v]—vi; *Dedication*, verso blank; Text, including Fly-titles, pp. [1]—[224]. Headlines throughout.   There   are   54   poems, including the Dedication.

Signatures : 4 leaves, unsigned; A—O, by 8s.

Issued in claret-coloured buckram lettered in gold : on back, *New / Poems / Francis / Thompson / Constable / Westminster*; on front cover, *New Poems / [Ornament] / Francis Thompson.*

Published price, 6s.

(162)

[VICTORIAN ODE : 1897]

Victorian Ode / For Jubilee Day, 1897, / By / Francis Thompson. / [*ornament*]

Collation : Foolscap octavo, 6¾ × 4⅜; pp. 16; consisting of Title-page as above, verso, *Printed for private circulation at the Westminster Press, 1897.*; Text pp. [3]—14; pp. [15]—[16], blank.

There are no signatures.

Issued in light grey wrappers, replica in red of the title-page on the front cover; on back cover reproduction of *No. 47. Palace Court.*

(163)

[HEALTH AND HOLINESS : 1905]

Health & Holiness / A Study of the Relations between / Brother Ass, the Body, and / his Rider, the Soul / By / Francis Thompson / With a Preface by / The Rev. George Tyrrell, S.J. / Burns & Oates, Ltd. / 28 Orchard Street, London, W. / 1905

Collation : Foolscap octavo, 6¾ × 4¼; pp. 80; consisting of Half-title, *Health and Holiness*, verso, Notice; Title-page, as above, verso blank; a Quotation, verso blank; *Preface*, pp. [viii]—x; Text, pp. [11]—80, imprint at foot, *Printed by Ballantyne, Hanson & Co. Edinburgh & London.* Each page is enclosed within a thin ruled border. Headlines throughout : first, *Preface*; then, *Health and Holiness*.

Signatures : [A], 4 leaves; B—E, by 8s; F, 4 leaves.

Issued in tan boards lettered in red on front cover within a red ruled border, *Health and / Holiness / A Study of the Relations between / Brother Ass, the Body, and / his Rider, the Soul / By / Francis Thompson / With a Preface by / The Rev. George Tyrrell, S.J.* Also issued in cloth.

Published price : boards, 1s; cloth, 2s.

* * *

ODE TO ENGLISH MARTYRS: 1906. This is a reprint; but the first separate edition.

* * *

(164)

[SELECTED POEMS : 1908]

Selected Poems / of Francis Thompson / London / Methuen and Co. Burns and Oates / Essex Street Orchard Street / W.C. W / 1908

Collation : Foolscap octavo, 6¾ × 4⅜; pp. xx + 144; consisting of Half-title, verso blank; Frontispiece; Title-page, as above, verso blank; *The Contents*, pp. v—vi; *A Biographical Note*, pp. vii—xvi; p. [xvii], blank; Dedicatory Poems, pp. xviii—xix, verso blank; Text, pp. 1—132; p. [133], blank, verso, ornament; *Appreciations*, pp. 135—142; Advertisements, p. [143], verso, *At the Arden Press, Letchforth.* Various headlines. There are 48 poems, including the Dedications.

Signatures : Ten leaves, unsigned; 1—9, by eights.

Issued in tan buckram lettered in gold : on back, *Selected / Poems / [Ornament] / Francis / Thompson,* [Ornament] ; on front cover, *Selected / Poems /* [Ornament] */ Francis Thompson* within gilt ruled border. Top edge gilt.

Published price, 5s.

The Biographical Note appeared in *The Athenæum* for *Nov. 23, 1891*, under the signature of *Wilfrid Meynell. To Olivia*, p. 105, is omitted from later issues. Page XI is misnumbered (X).

(165)

[HOUND OF HEAVEN: 1908]

The Hound / of Heaven / By Francis / Thompson / Burns and Oates / 28 Orchard Street / London / W

Collation: Foolscap octavo, 6⅝ × 4½; pp. 16 + 6; consisting of Half-title, verso blank; Title-page, within black ruled border, as above, verso blank; *A Note*, by Wilfrid Meynell p. [v], verso blank; Text, pp. 7—15, verso blank; Notices, 4 pp.; 2 pp. blank. Headlines throughout, *The Hound of Heaven.*

Issued in cream coloured boards, lettered in tan on front cover within decorative borders—*The / Hound / of / Heaven /* [Ornament] */ Burns and Oates / 28 Orchard Street / London / W*

Published price, 1s.

First separate edition.

(166)

[HOUND OF HEAVEN: 1914]

The Hound of Heaven / Ten Drawings for the Poem of Francis Thompson / By Frideswith Huddart / = / = / London / Chatto & Windus / 1914

Collation: Quarto, 12 × 9¾; 4 pp. of Text; ten mounted illustrations.

Issued in tan boards backed with buckram; lettered in gold on front cover, *The Hound of Heaven*; tan end papers.

First illustrated edition.

(167)

[SHELLEY: 1909]

Small paper copy:

Shelley / By Francis Thompson / With an Introduction / By the Rt Honble / George Wyndham / Burns and Oates / 28 Orchard Street / London W / 1909

Collation: Tall octavo, 7½ × 4⅝; pp. 92 + iv pp. adv.; consisting of Half-title *Shelley / By Francis Thompson*, verso blank; Title-page as above, within ruled black border, verso blank; Dedication, verso *First Edition*; *The Contents*, verso blank; Text, pp. 9—91, verso *Letchworth: At the Arden Press*; iv numbered pages adv. Headlines throughout, *Shelley*.

Signatures: [A]—F, by 8s.

Issued in olive green cloth lettered on back in gold, lengthwise; at foot, *By Francis / Thompson*; at top, *Shelley*; on the front within ruled gold border, *Shelley By Francis / Thompson.*

Published price, 2s 6d.

Large paper copy:

Shelley / By Francis Thompson / With an Introduction / By the Rt Honble / George Wyndham / Burns & Oates / 28 Orchard Street, London, W. / 1909

Collation : Royal octavo, $8\frac{1}{2} \times 5\frac{1}{2}$; pp. 94; consisting of Half-title, *Shelley / By Francis / Thompson*, verso blank; Title-page as above in red and black within one line red border; Dedication, verso blank; balance of the collation follows that of the small paper copy with the addition of a blank leaf.

Issued in cream coloured parchment boards lettered in gold on back as small paper copy. On front cover, within one line gold border, *Shelley* / [Ornament] / *By Francis / Thompson.*

(168)

[ST. IGNATIUS LOYOLA : 1909]

Saint / Ignatius Loyola / By Francis / Thompson / Edited by / John Hungerford Pollen, S.J. / With 100 Illustrations / By H. W. Brewer & Others / [*Facsimile*] / The Saint's Signature / Burns & Oates / 28 Orchard Street / London / W / 1909

Collation: Oblong Quarto, 9 × 5¾; pp. viii + 328; consisting of Half-title, *Saint / Ignatius Loyola*, verso blank; Approvals, verso, Frontispiece, within red border; Title-page, as above, in red and black, verso, Dedication; *Preface*, by Wilfrid Meynell, pp. [vii—viii]; Text, pp. 1—326, imprint at foot, *Printed by Ballantyne & Co. Limited Tavistock Street, Covent Garden, London*; p. [327], Ornament and Description, verso advertisements. Headlines throughout, *The Life of St. Ignatius*.

Signatures: 4 leaves, unsigned; A—2S, by fours.

Issued in dark green cloth, lettered in gold; on back, *Saint / Ignatius / Loyola / By / Francis / Thompson*; on front cover, *Saint / Ignatius Loyola / [Facsimile] / By / Francis Thompson*; gilt ruled border on back and on front cover. Top edge gilt.

Published price, 10s 6d.

(169)

[Eyes of Youth : 1909]

Eyes of Youth / *A Book of Verse by Padraic Colum · Shane / Leslie · Viola Meynell · Ruth Lindsay / Hugh Austin · Judith Lytton · Olivia / Meynell · Maurice Healy · Monica / Saleeby & Francis Meynell · With / four early Poems by Francis / Thompson, & a Foreword by /· Gilbert K. Chesterton.* / Herbert & Daniel / 21 Maddox Street / London / W.

Collation: Crown octavo, 7⅝ × 5⅛; pp. 6 + x + 96; consisting of blank leaf; Motto, verso blank; Title-page as above in red and black; verso blank; Note, verso blank; *Contents*, pp. [iii—v], verso blank; Foreword, pp. vii—x; Text, including Fly-titles, pp. [1]—94; Advertisements, pp. [95], verso *Printed by the Westminster Press Gerrards Ltd 411a Harrow Road, W.*

There are no signatures.

Issued in blue boards backed with tan buckram; a paper label on back reads *Eyes / of / Youth*; one on front cover, *Eyes of / Youth* within double ruled border.

Published price, 3s 6d.

About ten copies were bound for presentation in full vellum lettered in gold on front cover, *Eyes of / Youth.*

(170)

[RENEGADE POET: Boston, 1910]

A / Renegade Poet / and Other Essays / By / Francis Thompson / With an Introduction by / Edward J. O'Brien / [*Small ornament*] / Boston / The Ball Publishing Co. / 1910

Collation : Post octavo, 6⅝ × 4⅜; pp. 346 + vi; consisting of 2 pp. blank; Title-page as above, verso notice of copyright; *Table of Contents*, verso blank; *Introduction*; pp. 7—23, verso blank; Text, pp. 25—344; p. [345], Note, verso, advertisements; 6 pp. blank. Headlines throughout; verso, *A Renegade Poet*, recto various.

There are no signatures.

Issued in green cloth, lettered in gold; on back, *A /
Renegade / Poet / and Other / Essays / — / Thompson
/ Ball Pub. Co.*; on front *A Renegade Poet / and Other
Essays / Francis Thompson*; top edges gilt.

Published price, $1.25.

(171)

[WORKS : 1913]

The Works of / Francis Thompson / Poems :
Volume I [*II; Volume III: Prose*] / Burns &
Oates Ltd / 28 Orchard Street / London W

Collation : 3 Vols. Demy octavo, 8 × 5½.

Vol. I. : pp. xvi + 232; consisting of pp. [i—iv], blank;
Half-title, *The Works of / Francis Thompson /
Poems: Volume I,* verso blank; Frontispiece; Title-
page as above in red and black, verso blank; *A Note*
by Wilfrid Meynell, verso blank; *The Contents,* pp.
[xi—xiii], verso blank; *Dedication of Poems,* verso
blank; Text including Fly-titles, pp. [1]—226;
p. [227], Ornament, verso *Printed in England at the
Arden Press*; pp. [229-232] blank. Headlines
throughout.

Signatures : [A]—P, by 8s; Q, 4 leaves.

Vol. II. : pp. xvi + 232 + 8; consisting of pp. [i—vi]
blank; Half-title, etc., follow Vol. I. Text, pp. [1]—
[231], verso imprint; 8 pp. advertisements.

Signatures : [A]—Q, by 8s.

Vol. III. : pp. xvi + 296 + viii + 4; consisting of 3
blank leaves; Half-title, Frontis., Title-page, as in

former vols.; *The Contents*, pp. [xi—xii]; Preface, pp. [xiii—xiv]; *Motto*, verso blank; Text, pp. 1—291, verso blank; Acknowledgment, verso imprint; pp. [295—6], blank; Advertisements, viii pp.; 4 pp. blank. Various headlines throughout.

Signatures: [A]—U, by 8s; 2 leaves, unsigned.

Issued in tan buckram lettered in gold: on back, *The Works / of / Francis / Thompson / Volume I* [II, III]; on front cover, *The Works of / Francis Thompson /* [Ornament] */ Poems: Volume I.* [*II.; Prose: Volume III*]. Top edge gilt.

Published price, 6s per volume.

Special Edition:

The Works of / Francis Thompson / Poems: Book I [*etc.*] / London / Printed For F.M.W.M. / May, 1913

Collation: Royal octavo, $8\frac{1}{8} \times 5\frac{3}{8}$; three volumes, printed throughout on India paper, bound in one volume.

Issued in brown morocco binding; on back, *F.T.* in gold.

Of this edition 15 copies were printed for private presentation.

(172)

[EVERARD MEYNELL: Life of Thompson: 1913]

The Life of / Francis Thompson / By Everard Meynell / Burns & Oates Ltd / 28 Orchard Street / London, W / 1913

Collation: Demy octavo, 8¾ × 5½; pp. 4 +xii + 364 + 4;
consisting of 4 blank pages; Half-title, *The Life of
/ Francis Thompson,* verso blank; Frontispiece;
Title-page, as above, in red and black, verso blank;
To Grazia, verso blank; Acknowledgement, verso
blank; *Contents,* verso blank; *Illustrations,* verso
blank; Text, pp. [1]—361, imprint at foot *Printed
by Ballantyne Hanson & Co. At Paul's Work,
Edinburgh*; pp. [362—4], blank; 4 blank pages.
Various headlines throughout.

Signatures: 2 leaves, unsigned; [a], 6 leaves, A—Y,
by 8s; Z, 6 leaves; 2 leaves, unsigned.

Issued in tan buckram lettered in gold: on back *The
Life / Of / Francis / Thompson / Burns & / Oates
Ltd.*; on front cover, *The Life of / Francis Thompson
/* [Ornament] */ Everard Meynell.*

Published price, 15s.

Letters, etc. of Francis Thompson are here first
published.

(173)

[COLLECTED POETRY: 1913]

The / Collected Poetry / of Francis Thompson /
Hodder & Stoughton / London / MCM / XIII

Collation: Royal octavo, 9⅝ × 6¾; pp. xx + 416;
consisting of p. [1], blank, verso, Notice of Limitation; Half-title, *The Collected Poetry / of Francis
Thompson /* [Ornament, in pale blue], verso blank;
Title-page, as above, in pale blue and black, verso
blank; *Publishers' Note,* verso blank; *Contents,* pp.

ix—[xx] ; Text, including Fly-titles, pp. [1]—413;
verso, *Printed by T. and A. Constable, Printers to his
Majesty at the Edinburgh University Press*; pp.
[415—6], blank. Headlines, varying with Text.

Signatures : [a] and b, 4 leaves; c, 2 leaves; A—3F,
by 4s.

Issued in sky blue boards backed with tan linen; paper
label on back reads *The / Collected / Poetry of / Francis
/ Thompson /* [Ornament] */ Hodder & / Stoughton*;
front cover bears at top a printed label reading *The
Collected Poetry / of Francis Thompson* and a printed
Ornament at foot.

Published price, 20s.

2500 copies of this edition were printed.

Edition de luxe of 500 copies:

Royal octavo, 10⅛ × 7⅛. The collation agrees with that
of the Small Paper Copy except in the different
reading of the Notice of Limitation on p. [ii], which
is signed by the publisher and printer, and the added
frontispiece which is an *Etched portrait of Francis
Thompson, by H. Macbeth Raeburn.* Headlines and
signatures as in the Small Paper Copy.

Issued in limp vellum, with blue ribbon ties, lettered,
under gold ornament, on back, as in Small Paper Copy;
on the front, under gold ornament, *The Collected Poetry
/ of / Francis Thompson.*

Edition de luxe of 100 copies:

Royal octavo, 10½ × 8. Collation as edition of 500 copies
save for the addition of *10 pages of facsimiles* of
poems of Francis Thompson.

Issued in blue morocco backed with brown morocco, ornamented and tooled in gold, and lettered in gold within tooled border on the back only, *The / Collected / Poetry of / Francis Thompson.*

(174)

[SIR LESLIE STEPHEN : 1915]

Sir Leslie Stephen / As a Biographer. / By / Francis Thompson.

Collation : Quarto, 9⅛ × 7⅝; pp. 12; consisting of Title-page, as above, within ruled border, verso Notice of Limitation; Text, pp. [3—12].

Issued in stiff red wrappers; on the front cover is reproduced the title-page.

Of this edition, 20 copies were privately printed by Clement Shorter.

(175)

[MEYNELL : Who Goes There? : 1916]

Who Goes There? / *By the Author of / " Aunt Sarah & the War "* / Burns & Oates, Ltd. / 28 Orchard Street / London / W

Collation : Crown octavo, 7⅜ × 4⅝; pp. 96; consisting of Half-title, Title, Contents, Note, etc.

Issued in white wrappers lettered in black, and ornamented in red. Also in blue cloth gilt.

Published price : cloth, 2s 6d; paper, 1s.

This is My Beloved by Thompson appears on page 93 and is here published for the first time.

(176)

[UNCOLLECTED VERSE: 1917]

Uncollected / Verses / By / Francis Thompson / London / Privately Printed By Clement Shorter / July 1917

Collation : Demy octavo, 10 × 7⅜; pp. ii + 22; consisting of blank leaf; Half-title, *Uncollected Verses*, verso blank; Title-page, as above, within one line ruled border, verso Note of Indebtedness; Text, pp. 5—19, verso Notice of Limitation.

There are no signatures.

Issued in red wrappers; on the front cover is reproduced the title-page.

20 copies were printed for private distribution.

(177)

[THE MISTRESS OF VISION: 1918]

The / Mistress of Vision / By Francis Thompson / [*rubicated ornament*] / Together with / A Commentary / By the / Rev. John O'Connor S.T.P. / and with a / Preface by Father Vincent McNabb, O.P. /—/ Published by Douglas Pepler, Ditchling, Sussex. A.D. MCMXVIII

Collation : Quarto, 10⅝ × 7¼; pp. viii + 24 + viii; consisting of 5 pp. blank, verso, Notice of Indebtedness; Title-page, as above, verso blank; Text, pp. 1—23, verso, imprint; p. [i], blank; Advertisements, pp. [ii—iii] pp. [iv—viii] blank. Printed on laid paper.

There are no signatures.

Issued in black wrappers lettered in gold *The / Mistress of Vision / A Commentary / By the / Rev John O'Connor S.T.P.*

Published price, 5s.

First separate edition.

(178)

[LITTLE JESUS : 1920]

Little Jesus / [*design*] / Francis / Thompson

Collation : Octavo, 8 × 4⅞; pp. 12; consisting of 3 pp. blank, verso Latin Motto; Text, with Illuminations, pp. [5]—[9], verso blank; Notice of Artist and Publisher, p. [11], verso blank.

Issued, without a title-page, in peach coloured wrappers. The front cover (within double ruled border) has been described in lieu of title.

· There is an edition de luxe issued for presentation, differing from the Small Paper Copy only in two points. The size is 8⅜ × 5⅛, and the sides are bound at top and bottom by pieces of green satin ribbon.